Ale  **tu** |

Contemporary Film Directors

Edited by James Naremore

The Contemporary Film Directors series provides concise, well-written introductions to directors from around the world and from every level of the film industry. Its chief aims are to broaden our awareness of important artists, to give serious critical attention to their work, and to illustrate the variety and vitality of contemporary cinema. Contributors to the series include an array of internationally respected critics and academics. Each volume contains an incisive critical commentary, an informative interview with the director, and a detailed filmography.

A list of books in the series appears at the end of this book.

Alejandro González Iñárritu |

Celestino Deleyto and
María del Mar Azcona

UNIVERSITY
OF
ILLINOIS
PRESS
URBANA
CHICAGO
SPRINGFIELD

Frontispiece: Alejandro González Iñárritu

Library of Congress Cataloging-in-Publication Data
Deleyto, Celestino.
Alejandro González Iñárritu / Celestino Deleyto and María del Mar Azcona.
p. cm. — (Contemporary film directors)
Includes filmography.
Includes bibliographical references and index.
ISBN 978-0-252-03569-2 (cloth : alk. paper)
ISBN 978-0-252-07761-6 (pbk. : alk. paper)
1. González Iñárritu, Alejandro, 1963—Criticism and interpretation.
2. González Iñárritu, Alejandro, 1963—Interviews.
3. Motion picture producers and directors—Mexico—Interviews.
I. Azcona, María del Mar. II. Title.
PN1998.3.G6566D46   2010
791.4302'33092—dc22 [B]   2010016577

Contents |

Considered by many critics as a trilogy, Alejandro González Iñárritu's first three feature films have burst onto the scene of early-twenty-first-century cinema. Released at the dawn of the new century, *Amores perros* (2000) inaugurated one more renaissance of Mexican cinema and effortlessly inscribed itself within the parameters of global art cinema. Although in many ways very different from each other and from their predecessor, *21 Grams* (2003) and *Babel* (2006) confirm the consistency of Iñárritu's filmic world and his ability to connect with a contemporary *Weltanschauung*. The Mexican filmmaker has become one of the most powerful voices in the cinema of the new century on the basis of only three films. At the time of this writing, his fourth feature, *Biutiful,* was in the last stages of postproduction and slated to be released in 2010.

While most of the creative team from his first three films collaborated on *Biutiful,* one key player was missing: the scriptwriter Guillermo Arriaga. Not long after the release of *Babel,* a bitter argument abruptly ended what had been a fruitful collaboration. The release of *The Burning Plain* (2008), Arriaga's first venture as director, revealed striking differences, in spite of a comparable narrative structure, with Iñárritu's three films, suggesting that the separation might constitute a new beginning for both filmmakers. It is impossible to speculate on the direction that the director's *oeuvre* is going to take in the future. In our interview with Iñárritu, he confirmed that *Biutiful* is a linear, single-protagonist story that focuses intensely on the main character's subjectivity and that it will have little to do, at least in conceptual and structural terms, with his earlier films. In any case, the impact of his output as a feature director and the sophistication, intricacy, and manifold reverberations of his first three filmic texts have proven sufficient to situate him at the forefront of world cinema.

Born in Mexico City in 1963, Iñárritu started as a deejay at a radio station while he studied filmmaking and wrote the musical score for several films. In the 1990s he worked for Televisa, Mexico's foremost television company, where he was one of its youngest producers. He then spent most of the decade making hundreds of TV commercials, as well as a short film, *Detrás del dinero* (1995), produced by Televisa and starring the Spanish singer Miguel Bosé. Iñárritu wrote and directed his own commercials and, in his own words, probably spent more time on the set than any other director. Seen in retrospect, this was a period of feverish activity that sharpened his cinematic skills in preparation for his film work of the next decade. Toward the end of the decade, he met Guillermo Arriaga during a project involving a series of one-minute films, with different protagonists and stories, all revolving around a single incident, in this case a fire. The series never materialized, but it gave the filmmakers the idea and the creative impulse to make *Amores perros.*

After the critical and commercial success of his first feature film, Iñárritu would return to work as a director of commercials in a very different project: a series of shorts commissioned by BMW from renowned directors, all starring Clive Owen as a driver, to appear on the Internet (later gathered in a promotional DVD for the car company). The series was called *The Hire,* and it featured filmmakers like John Frankenheimer, Wong Kar-wai, Guy Ritchie, and John Woo. Iñárritu's short, "Powder Keg," involved a war photographer in a Latin American country (Stellan Skarsgård) whom Owen's U.N.-drafted driver attempts to rescue from hostile territory. The open political commitment found in this short film reappears in the director's other important piece from between his first two feature films, his collaboration in the portmanteau movie *11'09"01— September 11* (2002). In this collection of shorts about the impact of the tragedy of the Twin Towers in different places around the world, Iñárritu's was perhaps the most radical: eleven minutes and one second of mostly black screen, with Gustavo Santaolalla's sumptuous and plaintive score taking center stage and, from time to time, flashes of light in the middle of the screen briefly showing people falling from the windows of the buildings. More effectively than many of the other short films, Iñárritu captures the darkness and dramatic absurdity of the event that launched twenty-first-century history but also had very painful direct and indirect consequences for many people around the world.

In spite of the remarkable interest of the rest of the director's output, this book is going to focus exclusively on his first three feature films. From our perspective, Alejandro González Iñárritu's privileged position as one of the most significant and influential directors of the new century rests on two pillars, both of which can best be perceived through an analysis of *Amores perros*, *21 Grams*, and *Babel*: his dimensions as a transnational artist and as a consummate practitioner of the multiprotagonist film. Starting with an intensely localized story about his native Mexico City that immediately connected with thousands of spectators around the world and contributed to the international visibility of recent Mexican cinema, he then crossed the northern border with a story set in an unspecified city of the southern United States. As the logical continuation of this journey, *Babel* took him to three continents and became an almost literal example of global cinema (Europe was dropped at some point but has since become the destination of his fourth film, *Biutiful*). The films are equally transnational in industrial terms. Iñárritu has strived to maintain his creative independence by diversifying production and distribution deals across the world. More importantly, the films, particularly *Babel*, tell transnational stories and feature characters whose ambiguous mobility makes them representative of twenty-first-century global phenomena.

Essential to his filmic embodiment of transnationality is the use of the conventions of the multiprotagonist genre and the deployment of scrambled narratives. In his three collaborations with Arriaga, Iñárritu took one of the most popular cinematic forms of recent decades and crucially contributed to its development with three filmic narratives that have in common a multiplicity of stories, characters, and points of view but are also very different from one another. The complex and resounding narrative structures of these films go hand in hand with a formal sophistication in which visual and acoustic elements, as well as resonant editing strategies, become a crucial part of the director's approach to the new genre.

In this respect, the contribution of Iñárritu's usual collaborators—the director of photography Rodrigo Prieto, the composer Gustavo Santaolalla, the sound designer Martín Hernández, the production designer

Brigitte Broch, and the editor Stephen Mirrione—should not be underestimated. Above all of them, the figure of Guillermo Arriaga looms large. His involvement in the three films from the very beginning and the crucial role played by their sophisticated narrative structures place him alongside the director as more than just the author of the scripts. In this book, however, we will not explore the specific contributions made by each filmmaker to the creative process; we will consider the finished products as the consequence of the combined work of a team of exceptional artists. Following decade-long debates on film authorship, the use of the label "Alejandro González Iñárritu" to refer to the origin of the meanings created by the movies is to some extent a matter of convention and convenience. At the same time, Iñárritu, as the director, is a very real presence behind the movies and the central force under whose leadership the input of Arriaga and the rest has come to fruition. Our book, therefore, remains the study of a singular filmmaker.

The structure of this volume attempts to capture the distinctiveness of the Mexican director's *oeuvre* and some of the reasons for its cultural centrality. We begin by situating Iñárritu within the history of Mexican cinema and culture in an effort to explore his ability to transcend national parameters. The multiprotagonist film, as a narrative, generic, and interpretative framework, permeates most of our analysis, which focuses on the representation of time and space within the structure of this genre. Since *Amores perros, 21 Grams,* and *Babel* are equally significant for their cultural reverberations and their filmic sophistication, our critical commentary attempts to offer a combination of theoretical speculation and contextualization and textual analysis, zeroing in on the dimensions of each text that we find most suggestive. In temporal terms, each film conveys cultural and social meanings in specific ways, from the enhancement of simultaneity to the scrambling of time and the expansion and contraction of our sense of chronology. These temporal manipulations allow us, in our first approach to *Babel*, to tease out part of the links between the movies and issues of globalization and contemporary identity. Our take on the deployment of space is more formal, and we concentrate on the use of specific strategies such as the wide angle, the bleach bypass, and editing in transitions. Again, the analysis of formal transitions in *Babel* leads us to the cultural relevance of the concept of the border, in its material and metaphoric dimensions, in

Iñárritu's films and, more generally, in our transnational society. Space and time are, therefore, the driving forces of our study. Among other considerations, they help us place Iñárritu as both a located and deterritorialized artist, a filmic icon of the beginning of the twenty-first century and a philosopher of the intensity and inevitability of timeless human emotions and passions.

Research for this book has been financed by the Spanish Ministry of Education (research project no. HUM2007–61183/FILO) and the Diputación General de Aragón (re. H12). We carried out our research at the libraries of the University of Zaragoza, the Filmoteca de Madrid, and the Margaret Herrick Library of the Academy of Motion Picture Arts and Sciences in Los Angeles. We would like to thank Javier Herrera at the Filmoteca and Linda Mehr at the Herrick for their help and generosity. Our stay in Los Angeles was partly underwritten by the research fund of the University of Zaragoza. We would also like to thank James Naremore for giving us the opportunity to write this book and Joan Catapano and the staff at the University of Illinois Press for their editorial help. Juan Suárez, Isabel Santaolalla, Chris Holmlund, and Glenn Man provided advice and assistance at various stages, and our student Julia Echeverría helped us with various aspects of the book. Contacting Alejandro González Iñárritu was no easy task. We are indebted to Elena Deleyto, Joaquín Oristrell, and Sandra Hermida, who were the first links in the chain. Isolda Patrón-Costas, Iñárritu's agent, was a model of efficiency, generosity, and patience, and Alejandro González Iñárritu overwhelmed us with his kindness, humaneness, and intelligence. We are truly grateful to both for making the interview possible. Finally, our special gratitude goes to Tamar Jeffers McDonald, who read our manuscript on ridiculously short notice and provided invaluable comments and advice from which the book has benefited enormously.

Alejandro González Iñárritu |

Of Times and Places
The Films of Alejandro González Iñárritu

Down Mexico Way

In *21 Grams*, sometime after the deaths of her husband and two daughters, Cristina (Naomi Watts) walks to the corner where they were run over by a truck and sits briefly on the curb, overwhelmed by grief (fig. 1). The film underscores the importance of the moment visually and acoustically: in the first shot of the sequence, a long take, the handheld camera follows the character along the street in a sustained close-up, circles around her when she reaches the spot, and nervously stands in front of her while she looks around as if lost. Two briefer shots show her sitting and looking at the road, and then the camera pans left, leaving her offscreen, and focuses on the empty road where the accident took place. While Gustavo Santaolalla's slow musical theme incorporates a strain of sad tango music, a sound bridge of Michael's (Danny Huston) last cell-phone message carries us to the end of the sequence: Cristina lying on her bed, first in close-up and then in an oppressive high-angle

Figure 1. Cristina overwhelmed by grief
and loneliness in *21 Grams.*

long shot, listening to her husband's words again and again. The stylistic articulation of the sequence, along with Watts's effective performance, forces spectators to feel the unbearable loneliness of the character after the deaths of her dear ones and her radical isolation from a world that has stopped making sense. Comparable close-ups and extreme close-ups of the three protagonists' faces abound throughout the film. Long shots, generally brief, constantly punctuate the narrative, emphasizing the barrenness and desolation, which can be felt so strongly at this point. This sequence may therefore be seen as a stylistic *mise-en-abyme* of the whole text.

Both stylistically and narratively, *21 Grams* is immediately recognizable as an early-twenty-first-century U.S. independent film. Indeed, the movie was produced by This Is That, Ted Hope's production company, and distributed by Focus Features, headed by James Schamus. Hope and Schamus cofounded Good Machine in the early 1990s and quickly turned it into one of the crucial players in the independent scene. Following the path of other independent companies, Good Machine was acquired by Universal Pictures, whose new "independent" branch was renamed Focus Features. Schamus stayed in the studio while Hope broke away, but both remained important figures within the now-reshaped field. *21 Grams* was representative of these developments at the beginning of the twenty-first century. In addition, the presence in the cast of such crossover actors as Naomi Watts, Sean Penn, Benicio del Toro, and even Danny Huston place the film firmly within "the discourse of independence." According to Yannis Tzioumakis, what had once literally been independent (films produced and distributed outside the Hollywood industry) evolved into a label to designate the more adventurous products of the specialized divisions of the majors and, more significantly, a specific way of speaking about certain movies (9–11). Iñárritu himself feels part of this discourse when he describes himself as an independent filmmaker (Wood 145), thus adding his name to a cinematic tendency that only makes full sense within the cinema of the United States and with reference to Hollywood. At first sight, then, *21 Grams* can industrially and stylistically be considered part of the independent scene, along with films released in the same year, such as *The Good Girl*, *Lost in Translation*, *Thirteen*, *The Station Agent*, *American Splendor*, or *Casa de los Babys*.

Yet the history of *21 Grams* began many months before as a story and a script written in Spanish to be filmed in Mexico with Mexican actors. The film was the second feature directed by Iñárritu, who, after the international success of *Amores perros,* had become, along with his fellow filmmakers Alfonso Cuarón and Guillermo del Toro and the actors Gael García Bernal and Salma Hayek, a symbol of the success, vitality, and strength of Mexican cinema at the beginning of the twenty-first century. If there is little doubt that the discourse of American independent cinema constitutes an appropriate context for the study of a film like *21 Grams*, is the recent history of Mexican cinema another such context? Can the film usefully be seen not only as an instance in the career of its director but also as bearing specific resonances of his national culture? In more general terms, is this film, and its director's *oeuvre* as a whole, representative of larger trends within contemporary cinema? In this section we would like to look at the films of Alejandro González Iñárritu in their national context. We will interrogate the validity of the concept of Mexican national cinema and explore the extent to which the texts originate from and illuminate the extremely porous nature of that concept. As a necessary corollary, we will point at the ways in which they relate to the much debated but central notion of *mexicanidad.*

National identity has been the lynchpin of contemporary discussions of Mexican cinema. For Ernesto Acevedo-Muñoz, *Amores perros* and Cuarón's *Y tu mamá también* (2001) illustrate, along with other films of the same period, the crisis of national specificity in commercial world cinemas and the neutralization of culturally specific topics. Yet they continue to show an inherent *mexicanidad* in their treatment of gender relations (39–40). Similarly, Hester Baer and Ryan Long argue that Cuarón's film partakes of the tropes of global cinema but also incorporates specifically Mexican discourses (150–51). As in the case of these two films, debates on contemporary Mexican cinema revolve around the tension between national and transnational cinema, both from an industrial and a cultural perspective. Chon Noriega (Introduction xii–xiv) and Andrea Noble (23) believe in the continuing viability of the concept of Mexican national cinema, while Joan Hershfield fears its eventual disappearance in the face of a world dominated by migrations, deterritorializations, and reterritorializations (286). In a later book, Hershfield and David Maciel again wonder with concern how Mexican cinema can remain specifically Mexican while reaching a transnational audience (Epilogue 291).

However, in the same book, Ann Marie Stock counters that in a transnational world, "authentic national films" exist only as "distorting fictions" ("Authentically" 279). More specifically, in the conclusion to an earlier analysis of del Toro's *Cronos* (1993) as a film on migrancy and hybridity, Stock takes issue with critical distinctions between the authentic and the inauthentic in terms of national identity. She calls for a film criticism that understands postnational filmic practices that do not privilege origins, purity, and closure ("Migrancy" 161). For other writers, recent developments suggest that the national and the transnational need not be incompatible. Carl J. Mora argues that the young Mexican filmmakers of the 1990s seemed comfortable about maintaining their national and cultural identity even though this sense of identity had become more complex, sophisticated, and international (255). Sergio de la Mora sees in the same period similar attempts to rearticulate the national discourse of *mexicanidad* to produce an exportable image of modern Mexico for business and tourism, one no longer tied up with the macho mythology of the revolution (137). Whatever the diagnosis, critical and academic discourse on Mexican cinema remains firmly centered on the issue of national identity and the effects on it of transnational and global processes.

Where can the films of Alejandro González Iñárritu be placed within these debates? Do they represent a rethinking of Mexican identity for the twenty-first century, or are they illustrations of the crisis of national cinemas and, more generally, of the national as a cultural concept? When *Amores perros* came out, it was hailed not only as initiating a new renaissance of Mexican cinema but also as offering a radically different image of its country. This is how it was described by Lorenza Muñoz in the *Los Angeles Times*: "Picture a Mexico where young punks blare *rock en español* from their GMC trucks, yuppies drive BMWs to fancy hotels for afternoon trysts with their mistresses, thugs with spiked hair hold up local supermarkets, vicious dogs prowl the streets looking for prey, eking out a meager existence in their quest for survival. No strolling mariachis. No cactuses. No sombreroed *bandidos* drinking tequila. No Indian peasants smiling meekly—images of Mexico usually seen on the big screen" (10). Not exactly an exportable image of modern Mexico, as de la Mora argues, thinking no doubt of the great box-office success of the 1990s, *Como agua para chocolate* (Like water for chocolate; 1992). Yet the movie spoke to a country eager to shed some of its most traditional signifiers and to an international audience that, while discerning national specificities, could recognize some of the conflicts, social problems, and individual anxieties represented in the movie as no different from their own.

Opening only a couple of weeks before the political party in power, the PRI, lost the general elections for the first time in more than seventy years, the film was immediately seen as a symptom of a Mexican society pushing for change, its success at the box office partly a consequence of a craving for cultural texts that captured the new mood of the nation (Christopher 15; Smith, *Amores* 16–27). Its picture of a city plagued by kidnappings, murders, poverty, and homelessness has been related to the social consequences of the signing of the North American Free Trade Agreement (NAFTA) in the 1990s, but so has its box-office success (Morales 126). The movie therefore was framed within the context of economic changes brought about by a treaty that after a few years of existence had already transformed the face of the country (Saldaña-

Portillo 754–55). More specifically, Baer and Long have argued that the decline of state subvention for national cinemas has led to the emergence of privately and then globally funded films in a country like Mexico, where official funds had constituted the backbone of successive waves of art cinema (150).

Amores perros has been seen as a privileged example of this tendency. The film was as successful abroad as it was in Mexico, and Iñárritu was soon seen as part of a new generation of filmmakers that also included his friends Cuarón and del Toro. These directors were capable of making films that appealed not only to local spectators but also to a more international audience, not only to the festival circuit but to wider and more mainstream segments of the public as well. Unlike the previous generation, they found state-run film production crippling and looked for funding elsewhere.

Their films also reflect a more elusive attitude toward national identity. The older generation—Arturo Ripstein, Felipe Cazals, Jorge Fons, Jaime Humberto Hermosillo, and Paul Leduc, among others—had emerged during the Luis Echeverría sexenio (1970–76) and had produced an impressive body of work, which, under the influence of 1970s auteur cinema, had revitalized Mexican cinema after the profound crisis of the 1960s. In a cinema characterized by the constant search for a filmmaking form to express what is particular to the Mexican experience, this group of directors successfully redefined the concept of mexicanidad (Ramírez Berg 3, 44–45). The films of Arturo Ripstein, the best-known of the group, came to represent this cultural shift and became regular fixtures in festivals and art cinemas in Europe and the United States in the 1970s and 1980s, while remaining fiercely marginal and disconnected from the tastes of more mainstream audiences. When state funding stopped being forthcoming, Ripstein managed to continue making his "little" films, but most of the others encountered insurmountable problems. For Ramírez Berg, Mexican cinema at the start of the 1990s was facing no less than complete obliteration (217).

A late instance and one of the most celebrated works of this group of filmmakers, Jorge Fons's El callejón de los Milagros (Midaq Alley; 1995) shows that what may at the time have looked like the end of the road was instead a moment of transition toward a radically different era. Released the year after the signing of NAFTA, the movie was mostly state financed. In its depiction of sordid life in a dark, forgotten street in a poor district of Mexico City and of the mostly sexual anxieties and frustrations of its various inhabitants, it is representative, both formally and thematically, of its director's generation. At the same time, its multi-protagonist cast featured the relatively unknown Salma Hayek, who also starred in Robert Rodríguez's *Desperado,* released in the same year, a film with which she had started her climb toward Hollywood stardom, paving the way for similar border crossings. Hayek's attitude was shared by several young filmmakers, whose approach to their national cinema was radically different from that of the older generation.

After the small success of his state-funded *Sólo con tu pareja* (1991), Cuarón went to Hollywood, where he made the children's film *The Little Princess* (1995) and then a free adaptation of *Great Expectations* (1998) with Gwyneth Paltrow, Ethan Hawke, and Robert de Niro. He then returned to Mexico for the resounding critical success of *Y tu mamá también,* a short-lived visit that was followed by the Hollywood block-buster *Harry Potter and the Prisoner of Azkaban* (2004) and *Children of Men* (2006). Guillermo del Toro followed a similar, if more prolific, path. Working within the more consistent generic parameters of the fantasy-horror–science-fiction film, he came to public attention in his country with *Cronos* and immediately crossed the border to the United States to direct Mira Sorvino in *Mimic* (1997). These were followed by increasingly big-budget science-fiction Hollywood films—*Blade II* (2002), *Hellboy* (2004), and *Hellboy II: The Golden Army* (2008)—and two Mexican-Spanish coproductions, both set during the Spanish Civil War: *El espinazo del diablo* (The devil's backbone; 2001) and *El laberinto del fauno* (Pan's labyrinth; 2006). While both directors have engaged in big-budget mainstream ventures, perhaps their most characteristic offerings are films like *Y tu mamá también, Children of Men,* or *El laberinto del fauno,* features with an eye on the box office but equally appealing to more demanding audiences and critics, who can view at least some of them as instances of art cinema. Something similar can be said of Iñárritu's much shorter career. After the Mexican *Amores perros* and the U.S. *21 Grams, Babel* was technically a U.S-French-Mexican coproduction but in fact a film of uncertain nationality, while his next project, *Biutiful,* still unreleased at the time of writing, is a Mexican-Spanish coproduction.

It is significant that the three filmmakers who spearheaded Mexican cinema at the beginning of the twenty-first century have worked largely outside Mexico and, by the look of it, plan to continue to do so. Responding to attacks on his decision to make *21 Grams* in the United States, Iñárritu reasserted his right to make films abroad and his Mexicanness: "I am a very proud Mexican and I feel even more Mexican the further I go from my country. . . . It is a great thing for an artist to travel, because it gives an even greater perspective of oneself and one's country. . . . Why is it that painters and writers can go and live and work in other countries but film-makers cannot?" (qtd. in Wood 142). Similarly, after the release of *Hellboy,* del Toro asserted: "I work where I am allowed to—be that Spain, Prague, or the U.S. Wherever I go, however, I am a Mexican filmmaker, and that is a fact that gets lost on the people who make these criticisms. They believe—in what is a form of ultimate racism—that if you leave then you are no longer 'one of us' and you're not going to come back" (qtd. in Wood 154). The filmmakers see no contradiction between their national identity and the nationality of their films, which to them is largely irrelevant. Do their films, then, still bear the imprint of their makers' national origin? Can movies like *Harry Potter and the Prisoner of Azkaban* or *Hellboy* help us to understand Mexican cinema?

Such border crossings are characteristic of transnational cinema, and the films and the figures of Iñárritu, del Toro, and Cuarón are privileged examples of this tendency. Early-twenty-first-century cinema abounds in such examples, from directors like Wong Kar-wai and Fernando Meirelles and performers like Juliette Binoche and Penélope Cruz to films like *Blindness* (2008) and *Agora* (2009). According to Elizabeth Ezra and Terry Rowden, the contemporary world is being articulated in these films "as a global system rather than as a collection of more or less autonomous nations" ("General" 1). Yet the very concept of transnational cinema would not make sense if national cinema had become an irrelevant notion. Ezra and Rowden acknowledge the continuing importance of the national, even within a type of cinema that seeks to transcend it but which, in so doing, still respects it "as a powerful symbolic force" ("General" 2). For Jeff Menne, the tenacious presence of national cinemas may be producing a global culture that is more heterogeneous and decentered than many had imagined (86–88). At the same time, transnational cinema expresses a desire to go beyond national narratives and to imagine a new form of cosmopolitanism within popular culture. The cinema, particularly Hollywood cinema, has always had a transnational vocation. According to Ana M. López and others, the history of Latin American cinema abounds in examples of border crossings and transnational cross-fertilizations, although these have often been obscured by an excessive focus on national cinemas (34). In Latin America and elsewhere, this trend has been intensified in recent years through cultural shifts and industrial practices. Interestingly, Ezra and Rowden equate *auteur* cinema of the kind epitomized by the Mexican directors of the 1970s with national and ethnic identity, underlining Ramírez Berg's insights on their cultural importance within a national paradigm. Conversely, in an exchange of letters to the editor of *Sight and Sound*, Paul Julian Smith describes *Babel* as a "transnational prestige picture" and argues that in films like this there is no trace of distinctive national traditions ("Tower" 96).

The national and the transnational need not be theorized as contradictory and/or incompatible concepts, as Smith implies. The filmmakers themselves see no such contradiction, whereas Ezra and Rowden, like other authors, continue to acknowledge the importance of the national at the heart of the transnational. After wondering what remains of national identities in a time of globalization, interculturalism, multinational coproduction, free-trade agreements, and regional integration, Néstor García Canclini concludes that today identity is also a coproduction. This author does not see a danger that nations and ethnicities will disappear. Rather, the problem is to understand how traditional forms of identity are reconstituted through processes of intercultural hybridization ("Will There" 255–56). The national may not be on its way out, as Arjun Appadurai predicted some time ago, but the media and different forms of migration, the two forces that he finds behind changes in modern subjectivity, are reshaping our idea of the national (19).

In the case of Mexico, these global shifts may acquire more specific meanings, since, according to various cultural critics, its sense of national identity has always been hybrid and tenuous. In their analysis of *Y tu mamá también*, Baer and Long argue that, in incorporating elements from both the Mexican cinematic tradition and global styles, the film reproduces the space occupied by the country itself, halfway between the local and the global (151). For María Josefina Saldaña-

Portillo, the Mexican sense of sovereignty is bookended by two treaties with its northern neighbor, separated by almost 150 years: the treaty of Guadalupe-Hidalgo, the legal resolution to an imperialist war waged against Mexico by the United States, as a consequence of which Mexico was dispossessed of half of its territory; and the NAFTA agreements (752–53). *Mexicanidad* became affected and permanently debilitated by the former and further diluted by the latter, its essence therefore framed by a deep-seated anxiety about its autonomy.

This anxiety, as argued in Octavio Paz's influential *El laberinto de la soledad* (The Labyrinth of solitude; 2003), can be traced back to before the war against the United States to the country's origins in the Spanish *conquista*. According to Paz, la Malinche, the native woman who betrayed the Aztecs and then became Cortés's lover, is one of the most powerful national archetypes because she represents Mexicans' will to condemn and renounce their hybrid origin. Mexicans do not want to be Indian or Spanish; they do not see themselves as *mestizos*, either, but rather as an abstraction, as motherless children with no origin, always looking elsewhere for an imaginary identity (224–25). The country's long and often traumatic history under the shadow of the northern neighbor may have increased this anxiety. At the same time, perhaps paradoxically, it may have placed it in a better position to assimilate recent cultural developments in which the national begins to lose ground to or at least to be redefined by the global and the transnational. Its identity having been historically shaped under the shadow of other identities, the national may in Mexico find it easier both to resist and incorporate the transnational, since its protracted and obsessive search for identity has been constantly marked by such resistances and incorporations. From a different perspective, it may not come as a surprise that a generation of filmmakers who represent a country eager to change and shed some of the ghosts of its past may be less obsessed with historical traumas and traditional forms of identity and more ready to embrace the transnational as a new way to define the national. Iñárritu's films can also be seen as a symptom of these changing attitudes.

Mexicanidad, the search for the imaginary essence of the national identity, has become a coproduction; in fact, it has always been one. Yet this does not invalidate its importance and its critical potential to explain contemporary Mexican cultural products. Iñárritu's movies emerge at the beginning of the twenty-first century not only from a specific industrial context but also from a cultural one in which the anxious search for the essence of national identity remains an important part. As follows from the title of his book, *El laberinto de la soledad,* for Octavio Paz the most representative trait of Mexican identity is solitude. In their incessant search for an origin, in their negation of historical origins, Mexicans are always enclosed in themselves, not open even to fellow Mexicans for fear of seeing their own reflection in them (155). Ramírez Berg takes up this idea to define Mexican cinema from 1967 to 1983 as a cinema of solitude—films that feature a parade of characters lost in their loneliness, metaphors of a country whose sociopolitical center has not held, leaving its citizens isolated and abandoned (2). This sense of isolation, however, may well go beyond the specific historical period described by this author.

In the scene from *21 Grams* described above, a series of sophisticated stylistic devices convey the character's excruciating feeling of isolation from the world around her. The handheld camera pans, circles, and tilts nervously, both cutting Cristina off from her surroundings and finding only empty spaces when it attempts to move beyond her body and follow her gaze. Back in her house, her previous life has become an unbearable weight that now defines her identity, an impression suggested by the extreme close-up of her reclining face and the oppressive high-angle shot emphasizing her loneliness that ends the sequence. In fact, Cristina is one of several solitary characters in the movie whose traumatic experiences have left them as isolated and abandoned as the figures described by Ramírez Berg, although for very different reasons. The film's structure facilitates parallels and reflections between the various experiences of suffering leading to isolation, turning the narrative into a hall of mirrors that enlarges individual meanings and identifies loneliness as the essence of the human condition.

This is not to suggest that the filmic representation of extreme solitude automatically makes the film representative of Mexican cinema. Loneliness and solitude have been explored by movies within many cinematic traditions. They are particularly familiar tropes in contemporary U.S. independent cinema, whose preference for the long static take, minimalist performance, and empty spaces is often related to the representation of states of isolation and seclusion from unfriendly or alienating surroundings. Yet it may be no coincidence that this "indie" production that narrates the predicament of a group of characters radically cut off from the world around them but also eager to transcend that condition and reach out for the others has originated from a Mexican story. Both the scriptwriter Guillermo Arriaga and the director have said that the film deals with universal feelings and experiences, which made it easy for them to transplant their story north of the border (Wood 144). But their story may also be seen as an exploration of the human condition carried out from a geographically specific perspective. This sense of isolation in the midst of an increasingly intercommunicated world is present also in *Amores perros* and especially in *Babel*.

21 Grams is an apparently pure exemplar of early-twenty-first-century U.S. independent cinema, but a closer look questions such purity. Its metaphorical journey from Mexico to the United States already calls our attention to its hybridity. Even its cast—which features an actor from Puerto Rico, another from Australia, one of mixed Anglo-French origin, and one Irish-American—intensifies this impression and inflects this "universal" story not only with a sense of the transnational but also with a very Mexican feeling of *mestizaje*. Although Paz asserts that Mexicans are always in denial of their *mestizo* origins, sociologists like Natividad Gutiérrez find that the *mestizo* is the most salient feature of *mexicanidad*. This feature, promoted and celebrated by the Mexican Revolution, refers not only to racial mixture but also to a fusion of cultures, traditions, and styles (88). The story of *21 Grams*, like those of other contemporary films, accommodates this national and cultural hybridity effortlessly. More generally, the smooth adaptation of a filmmaker like Iñárritu to a transnational cinema and his ability to situate himself at the forefront of this exciting new tendency may be closely linked to the cultural experience of a country that has had to cope with its own hybridity for centuries.

Death is at the narrative center of *21 Grams*—the deaths of Michael and his daughters, and the death of Paul (Sean Penn). Paul struggles with the looming presence and, increasingly, the inevitability of his own death, and the rest of the major characters have their lives drastically changed as a result of the car accident. The film's intricate narrative structure revolves around the two events that, if the scrambled narrative were to be reordered, would roughly constitute the beginning and end of the story. An awareness of death as omnipresent is again curiously close to Paz's description of the Mexican character. The well-known proximity of mortality in all sorts of cultural manifestations coming from Mexico was noted by Enrique Krauze in the *Los Angeles Times* as a way to explain the film's success in that country: "It is only natural. Indigenous Mexican culture and Hispanic culture both face death with a stoic familiarity that in some ways still colors contemporary Mexican life." Paz argues that for the Aztecs, life and death were a mere prolongation of each other; although this belief has been partly lost, it has not disappeared altogether. Whereas other cultures do not even dare name it, Mexicans show a certain indifference toward death: they frequent it, mock it, and sleep with it; it is one of their favorite toys and their most permanent lover. Mexicans are just as afraid as anybody else, but they do not hide from the inevitable (193).

It could be argued that in *21 Grams*, Iñárritu, the Mexican artist, attempts to export a culturally specific view of human mortality to the United States, which as a society prefers to push the reality of death away from everyday experience (Krauze), and to observe the result of the confrontation. The characters are initially devastated by the mortality that surrounds them, but they gradually come to terms with its presence as one more fact of their lives, and they come to incorporate it into their extraordinary capacity to survive through deeper forms of love and communication. In a very palpable sense, death also crosses the border with Iñárritu—it will take a more literal return journey two years later in Arriaga's script of *The Three Burials of Melquiades Estrada* (2005)—and, in making the leap, illustrates the complexity and fascination of the transnational cultural object.

In Mexico, death is particularly visible in their frequent fiestas, another stereotype of the national culture. For Paz, the Mexican fondness for all kinds of celebrations is not incompatible with but a consequence of the solitude, gloom, and reserve that define the national character. When the reticent Mexican opens up, he does so with a degree of excess and violence that is difficult to understand by other cultures. It is an expression of the mask that is permanently worn and always in danger of being torn off by a sudden explosion of intimacy (Paz 200). Paz therefore finds in the essential solitude of the national character the source of what from outside may be perceived as a cult of the excessive that pervades all sorts of social and cultural manifestations. The history of the country's cinema is one of those manifestations that is characterized by a rhetoric of excess.

Whether or not we accept the speculations of Octavio Paz and other cultural observers as to the reality of such elusive concepts as national character, the first impression of the newcomer to Mexican cinema is that it is a cinema of excess, particularly in the representation of desire and violence. Desire is openly incestuous in one of the key Mexican films of the 1930s, Arcady Boytler's *La mujer del puerto* (Woman of the port; 1933), and in Arturo Ripstein's 1991 remake, but various forms of "extreme" desire pervade most trends, periods, and generic configurations of the country's cinema history. Women suffer unspeakable humiliation and indignities in mainstream classical melodramas like *Las abandonadas* (The Abandoned; 1945), *Río Escondido* (Hidden river;1948), and *Aventurera* (1949). Unusual in comparison to other classical cinemas, in many of these melodramas the often convoluted action is interspersed with musical numbers, the Mexican penchant for excess showing even in the generic mixture. For example, *Nosotros los pobres* (We the poor; 1947), one of the most popular Mexican films ever, has the star singer Pedro Infante perform several songs in the midst of a very dark account of life among the poor that follows a daughter's search for her lost mother. This is a story packed with mirroring events and frequent coincidences that strain even the loosest standards of verisimilitude. *Allá en el Rancho Grande* (Out on the big ranch; 1948) is a remake of the film that in the previous decade inaugurated one of the country's most popular genres, the *ranchera*. Infante's box-office rival Jorge Negrete stars in a musical romantic comedy that includes a male character who would have paid one hundred pesos to sleep with his best friend's girlfriend and a stepmother who sells her Cinderella-like daughter to pay for her other daughter's wedding. The various forms of violence and excess that may be found in Luis Buñuel's Mexican films have often been attributed to the Spanish director's allegiance to the surrealist ethos; yet *Los olvidados* (1950), *Él* (1952), *El bruto* (1952), *Ensayo de un crimen* (The Criminal life of Archibaldo la Cruz; 1955), and others are as recognizably Mexican as the other films mentioned here in their ruthless attack on various social flaws.

Arturo Ripstein's oeuvre is well known for its treatment of extreme passions and his creation of morbid and grotesque cinematic worlds. In one of his lesser-known films, *La perdición de los hombres* (The Ruination of men; 2000), a man is killed by his two friends at the beginning of the narrative; his corpse remains onscreen for most of the story, while his murderers calmly discuss what to do with it, and the two women in his life fight over it. The black-and-white cinematography, the virtuoso use of the long take, and the fragmented narrative structure, among other filmic devices, may turn the film into art-house fare, but its excess is part and parcel of the history of national cinema. If *La perdición de los hombres* is a late example of the work of the directors who came to prominence during the Luis Echeverría sexenio, Luis Alcoriza's *Mecánica nacional* (National mechanics; 1972) was one of its first offerings. The extremity of Ripstein's perspective is equally apparent in this black-comedy indictment of Mexican machismo, which features a family's increasingly absurd attempts to dispose of their grandmother's corpse after she dies from overeating during a long, drawn-out, and very eventful picnic.

When *Amores perros* came out, its depiction of violence was immediately noticed by commentators and compared to the films of Buñuel and Ripstein (it was released in the same year as *La perdición de los hombres* but to much greater acclaim and audience visibility). For Marvin D'Lugo, Iñárritu had learned from those two masters that "the devastating portrait of visceral violence and fatalism" had become the most successful image of Mexico abroad (229). Claudia Schaefer pointed out that Iñárritu's refusal to cut away when showing moments of intense emotion or violence may make international spectators squirm, but Mexican society is apparently unshockable (86).

Buñuel and Ripstein may have been the most obvious models at hand, but Quentin Tarantino and *Pulp Fiction* (1994) were mentioned even more often in the United States, with less justification. Many other examples from the history of Mexican cinema, classical and modern, might have been more apt. Iñárritu's film does not break with the past, nor does it necessarily follow in the steps of the most reputable of its predecessors. In its often shocking depiction of a society in the constant grip of violence and in its ostensible wallowing in a rhetoric of excess, *Amores perros* places itself at the center of a long cinematic tradition. Predictably, other Mexican films immediately before and after it display the same approach: *Crónica de un desayuno* (A Breakfast chronicle; 1999), for example, shows a transvestite looking for the penis that a lover had cut off the previous night and discussing with a doctor the possibilities of sewing it back in. *De la calle* (Streeters; 2002) revisits the same territory as the first story of Iñárritu's film, substituting wrestling for dog fights. It tells the story of a young couple who dream of escaping to Veracruz from the Mexico City underworld in which they have always lived. They end up being raped, she by a corrupt policeman and he by his own transvestite father. Like Ripstein's films, *Soba* (2004) employs art-house devices such as black-and-white cinematography, pictorial compositions, and slow-paced editing to tell a story of torture, incest (the female protagonist has sex with her stepfather), gang rape by the police, and corruption. This film was released in the same year as *Batalla en el cielo* (Battle in heaven), the second feature directed by Carlos Reygadas, whose work is informed by the same rhetoric of excess. Reygadas is among the most egregious representatives of the boom in national cinema that followed the success of Iñárritu, Cuarón, and del Toro at home and abroad, and his films share in the same cultural tradition as its predecessors. In sum, the familiarity and proximity of death, the shocking violence, and the sustained reluctance to refrain from the representation of intense experience are not features that mark Iñárritu's originality but rather his cultural origins.

Not that the films described above were the only kind that could be found on Mexican screens at the end of the 1990s. *Como agua para chocolate,* the great success of the decade, had offered a very different perspective: softening the potentially disturbing edges of its magic-realist story of immortal love, it proved that Mexico could make movies that looked attractively local and whose specificity was not disconcerting for international audiences. Del Toro and Cuarón were making their first features around the same time. From a generic perspective, *Cronos* was a relatively isolated case in the decade, but the combination of comedy of manners and satirical and romantic comedy in Cuarón's first film, *Sólo con tu pareja,* remains much more popular in Mexico. *Sexo, pudor y lágrimas* (Sex, shame, and tears; 1999), the great box-office achievement of the decade at home, also deals with intimate matters among contemporary middle-class urban young couples and friends using a multiprotagonist structure. Such mainstream comedies have abounded in recent Mexican cinema, including *En el país de no pasa nada* (In the country where nothing happens; 2000), *Vivir mata* (Life kills; 2002), *7 mujeres, un homosexual y Carlos* (2004), *Desnudos* (2004), *La última noche* (2004), and *Cansada de besar sapos* (Tired of kissing frogs; 2006).

If *Amores perros* was soon associated with the new social climate that would eventually dislodge the PRI from power, a satirical comedy from the previous year, Luis Estrada's *La ley de Herodes* (Herod's law; 1999), tackled the issue more directly with a story about political corruption in the 1940s that would have been impossible to film in earlier periods of tighter government censorship (Maciel 52). A comparison with *Río Escondido* is illuminating: in the classical film, a teacher, Rosaura Salazar (María Félix), is sent to a remote village by the president of the republic to fight the corruption of the local *cacique*, which she does successfully; in the modern film, a mediocre member of the ruling party, played by Damián Alcázar, goes on a similar errand, only to become as corrupt and his predecessor. Police corruption is another national cliché that appears frequently in earlier Mexican movies. However, censorship, which had traditionally been uninterested in sex and violence, prevented any serious exploration of political corruption and its structural pervasiveness in the country's history.

Although not as well known as *Amores perros,* Estrada's film was a harbinger of changes to come. *La ley de Herodes* also reflects some of the variety of the contemporary panorama of Mexican cinema, which includes political thrillers like *Conejo en la luna* (Rabbit on the moon; 2004), horror films related to traditional myths like *Las lloronas* (2004) and *Kilómetro 31* (2007), and road movies like *Sin dejar huella* (Without a trace; 2000). Carlos Reygadas is one of several emerging directors catering for more or less minority tastes, and films like *Japón* (Japan; 2002) and *Stellet Licht* (Silent light; 2007) regularly play in the festival circuit to increasing international interest, along with those of other young filmmakers, like Rodrigo Plá's *La zona* (2007) and Fernando Eimbecke's *Temporada de patos* (Duck season; 2004) and *Lake Tahoe* (2008). Many of these films can be inscribed within the rhetoric of excess described above, but in other cases *mexicanidad* must be found elsewhere.

The wind of change was strongly felt in Mexico at the turn of the twenty-first century, and *Amores perros* encapsulated this feeling. Paul

Julian Smith has documented this historical dimension and has argued that, for all of the director's and scriptwriter's rejection of past national cinematic models, the film curiously fits Ramírez Berg's description of classical Mexican cinema (*Amores* 37). Even the new paths that it undeniably opened must be historically contextualized. For example, its international success beyond the art-house circuits that had welcomed the films of Ripstein and his contemporaries suggested the previously unexplored transnational potential of Mexican cinema. Yet this potential can be linked to specific elements of national identity such as the enduring, looming presence of the powerful northern neighbor. The film's very existence can be seen as a consequence of the implementation of the NAFTA agreement, but it does not cower from representing some of the social consequences of the country's new economic regime, including the growing pressures on the urban population of its sprawling capital caused by massive immigration from the impoverished rural areas. The hostility and aggressive instincts displayed by most of the characters in the first story can be linked to specific historical conditions and wider views of national identity. The dog fights have been seen as metaphors of the brutality of everyday human interaction in the country's capital, but they can equally work as signifiers of a more endemic violence.

The story of el Chivo (Emilio Echevarría) adds to this visceral quality to be found everywhere in Mexican cinema while also capturing a feeling of disenchantment with revolutionary ideals that were betrayed by those in power. This feeling is compounded by the routine presence of police corruption: the ex-guerrilla-fighter-turned-hired-assassin and the corrupt policeman are friends and even business associates. This strand of the plot also continues another well-established tradition of the country's cinema: the melodramatic vilification of the affluent classes. The polarized contrast between the poor and the rich, also a staple of classical Mexican cinema, is here reflected in the abrupt contrast between the first two narrative segments. Apart from censuring the superficiality and insincerity of the middle classes, the second narrative segment may be said to incorporate more surreptitiously some of the country's historical ghosts: the presence of the Spanish model Valeria (Goya Toledo) conjures images of the Spanish past and la Malinche, who betrayed the country to the foreign invader. Throughout the three stories, the visceral formal approach to representation and the visceral emotions represented return us to the rhetoric of excess that pervades many forms and tendencies of Mexican cinema. At the same time, like *El callejón de los Milagros* with Salma Hayek, *Amores perros* featured the newcomer Gael García Bernal, who would soon join the three transnational filmmakers and Hayek as the face of Mexican cinema for the first decade of the twenty-first century. The young star's later presence in films from various parts of the world further recontextualizes Iñárritu's first movie as local in its immediate interests and global in its reach, both national and transnational. In cinematic terms, the transnationality of *Amores perros* can be seen most clearly in its use of the new genre that the filmmaker's career as a whole has come to encapsulate at the outset of the twenty-first century: the multiprotagonist film.

Of Middles, Beginnings, and Endings

At the beginning of *Río Escondido,* Rosaura Salazar, a school teacher with a heart condition, arrives at the Palacio Nacional in Mexico City. As she ascends the majestic staircase of the presidential building, she looks in wonder at the history of her country on a mural painted by Diego Rivera. She has been summoned by the president of the republic, who is assigning a specific task to each individual as part of his national political project. Each individual matters, and the road to a better future for the country will not be built by a charismatic leader but by joint communal effort. The president's strategy mirrors the account of the history of Mexico envisioned in Rivera's crowded mural. The essence and the history of Mexico, the text seems to be arguing, cannot be reduced to a succession of historical moments but must be expanded to include the assortment of lives and stories brought by each of the figures found in this multiprotagonist mural. Regardless of their specific political goals, the packed and colorful portrayals of Mexican life by Diego Rivera and the Mexican muralists are among the most representative icons of the country's pictorial tradition and of its art in general. Although very different in terms of their ideological discourses, the broad canvases of characters and stories that are so characteristic of Iñárritu's films can be traced back to this tradition.

Form matters. Each story has and needs to find its own way of being told. "It's like everything else: Tequila you have to serve in a small glass, because the flavor is different if you serve it in a tall glass; or whiskey or champagne: they have their own form. And I think sometimes form is intrinsic to the essence of the thing" (Iñárritu qtd. in Littger 188). Comments of this sort were recurrent when Iñárritu and Arriaga were asked about the narrative structures of *Amores perros, 21 Grams,* and *Babel.* In their hands, the three movies found their own specific ways to be told—ways that, in spite of their similarities, differ from one movie to the next. The three films are structured around an accidental event whose effects branch off in different directions to weave a human tapestry of independent but interrelated lives. Random chance features in them not only as a triggering device that makes separate lives affect one another in unexpected ways but as a major thematic element looming over the films' fragmented narrative pattern. Rather than simply a vessel for the story, the form becomes an intrinsic part of it.

However closely linked form is with the content of the particular stories in Iñárritu's films, the human mosaics assembled by these three movies need to be placed in the context of the experimentation with multiple characters and narrative lines that took place at the end of the twentieth century and turned what had until then been just an alternative storytelling pattern into a proper genre with its own thematic concerns and narrative and visual conventions. Films with several protagonists have existed since the early years of classical cinema. D. W. Griffith's *Intolerance* (1916) was an early example of the structure, as were MGM's narrative experiments with a wide collection of stars in relatively self-enclosed milieus such as *Grand Hotel* (1932), *Dinner at Eight* (1933), and *The Women* (1939). Always an available and versatile alternative for filmic storytelling, the format, which was put to different but relatively isolated uses in the decades that followed, was especially prolific in the cycle of disaster movies of the 1970s and, for very different reasons, in the hands of Robert Altman, the first director who turned multiprotagonist films into his auteurist mark. A specific use of the format became popular in the 1980s, when certain movies started to build their stories around large ensembles of characters of similar narrative importance (usually friends or family members but also looser and more randomly connected groups), who brought with them particular storylines, ways of behavior, and attitudes, thus providing a panoply of points of view and insightful explorations of human interaction and group dynamics:

The Return of the Secaucus Seven (1980), *Diner* (1982), *A Midsummer Night's Sex Comedy* (1982), *Fast Times at Ridgemont High* (1982), *The Big Chill* (1983), *St. Elmo's Fire* (1985), *Hannah and Her Sisters* (1986), *Do the Right Thing* (1989), *Parenthood* (1989), and *Steel Magnolias* (1989), among others.

As the tendency made its way into the 1990s, it also became more sophisticated and varied. Spatially bound groups were sometimes replaced by a collection of more or less isolated individuals or couples scattered around a city or town whose paths and storylines crisscrossed in accidental and random ways, as in films like *Grand Canyon* (1991), *City of Hope* (1991), *Short Cuts* (1993), *Prêt-à-Porter* (1994), *Your Friends and Neighbors* (1998), *Magnolia* (1999), or *Go* (1999). The format gained momentum, versatility, and visibility in the years that followed: films like *Traffic* (2000), *Syriana* (2005), *Fast Food Nation* (2006), and *Babel* managed to move freely between characters and stories that took place in different countries or even continents. Within these movies' ever-widening geopolitical frameworks, their emphasis on human interaction and on random connections does not only affect individuals at a personal level but usually has broader social and political consequences. The success of *Crash* (2004) at the Academy Awards gave a symbolic seal of mainstream authority to the genre and proved its ability to deal with contemporary social concerns in ways that defy easy answers and oversimplification.

The current popularity of the genre is by no means restricted to U.S. cinema. It has become a transcultural phenomenon (Tröhler), and Mexican cinema is not an exception to the trend. More or less scattered examples, such as *Los Olvidados*, *Reportaje* (1953), and *Mecánica Nacional*, can be found in earlier decades, but since the 1990s, Mexican multiprotagonist movies have become more visible and have specialized in certain types of stories: life in a small community, usually in Mexico City, be it the remote street of *El callejón de los milagros* or the big apartment building of *Corazones rotos* (Broken hearts; 2001); the experience of emigration as seen from an assortment of perspectives in María Novaro's *El jardín del Edén* (The Garden of Eden; 1994), in which three women's lives come together in Tijuana, or in *Al otro lado* (2004), a film that tells three consecutive stories of children whose parents have emigrated to different countries; the hardships of life for the marginal and downtrodden in the big city, whether the members of a dysfunctional family in *Crónica de un desayuno* or a group of homeless teenagers eking out a living in the rough streets of *De la calle*; comic/satirical canvases of contemporary intimate matters like *Cilantro y Perejil* (Recipies to stay together; 1995), *Sexo, pudor y lágrimas*, and *La última noche*; or bittersweet tales of lonely lives that intercross in the big city, like *Cosas insignificantes* (Insignificant things; 2008).

Before and after the impact of *Amores perros*, the multiprotagonist format seems to be very much at home in contemporary Mexican cinema. Wide ensembles had been a favored storytelling option not only in the culturally prestigious packed human groups of the murals but also in the *telenovelas,* one of the most popular forms of entertainment in the history of Mexico that has always shamelessly indulged in the proliferation of characters, storylines, and points of view for melodramatic excess. Iñárritu's three feature films have been compared to this popular genre in terms of narrative arcs and ideological values (Smith, *Amores* 39) and often disparaged because of the similarity (Ayala 485; Quart 74; Denby 85). It has often been argued, for instance, that were it not for its unconventional narrative structure, *21 Grams* would be just a conventional melodrama and not the high-art product it pretends to be (Denby 84; Hoberman 64; Kerr 354; and Landesman 15).

Amores perros, 21 Grams, and *Babel* need to be seen in the context of the popularity, both national and international, of films that experiment with multiple characters and plotlines, but they also constitute specific manifestations of the genre. A common feature of the three films is the scrambling of linear time, whether by telling three roughly simultaneous stories in *Amores perros* consecutively instead of crosscutting between them; by freely moving between past, present, and future, as in *21 Grams*; or, as in *Babel,* by implying a false sense of simultaneity between different stories. When *Amores perros* came out, critics insistently related it to *Pulp Fiction* on the basis of its articulation of filmic time, a connection repeatedly denied by the director (Littger 190). Apart from the literary antecedents—Arriaga usually mentions William Faulkner when asked about his influences regarding the form of his stories (Arriaga, Introduction vii; Scott xvii)—there have been numerous examples of chronological fragmentation and proliferation of points of view throughout the history of cinema, from *Citizen Kane* (1941) to *A Letter to Three Wives* (1949) and *The Killing* (1956); from *Rashomon* (1950) to Alain Resnais's *Hiroshima mon amour* (1959), *L'Année dernière à Marienbad* (1961), and *Muriel ou le temps d'un retour* (1963), among many others. Iñárritu has specified his own influences in this respect: rock operas, Latin American fiction, and contemporary films like *Short Cuts* (1993), *Before the Rain* (1994), and *Smoke* (1995) (Lowenstein 84–85).

Iñárritu also sees a straightforward connection between the multiplicity of stories and the abandonment of linear narrative, two features that he regards as an intrinsic part of daily experience in our contemporary technological environment: "I think that we have been exposed to so many different media now—the kids are now basically dealing with three, four, five realities at the same time: they are watching CNN and are reading the treadmill at the bottom of the screen—then a friend calls from New York while they are receiving an e-mail from New Zealand. . . . And the virtuality that we are now living in makes our minds more prepared to deal with stories that are nonlinear—you can be playing with several realities" (qtd. in Littger 190). The narrative form of the films, therefore, is inspired as much by postmodern society as by other texts.

Yet it is undeniable that from the early 1990s there has been a renewal of interest in experimentation with temporal structures, and Iñárritu's films are also a consequence of that trend. This context is relevant to explain, for example, the films' reception by audiences that, as had happened before in the 1960s and 1970s, were becoming familiar again with such manipulations. At the same time, close attention must be given to the filmmaker's specific approach to time and the ways in which the temporal fragmentation of his multistranded plots allows him to convey certain attitudes toward society and interpersonal relationships. Iñárritu places time at the center of his preoccupations by combining the potential of the cinema as a "time machine" (Christie 33) with the flexibility and capacity for temporal manipulation of the multiprotagonist movie. Apart from this general interest in scrambled narratives, the structures of the three films are very different from one another—a logical consequence of the decorum that the director appears particularly concerned with: each drink needs its own glass. In this section, we look closely at the strategies employed to represent chronological and filmic time in the first two films: the importance of simultaneity in *Amores perros* and the apparent temporal confusion in *21 Grams*. These films show that time affects the characters and how spectators make sense of the stories in crucial ways and convey particular approaches to contemporary cultural phenomena, while at the same time zeroing in on Iñárritu's main fascination: the beauty of interpersonal relationships, the wonders of physical contact between human beings, and the power and fragility of human happiness.

Hall of Mirrors

The first words of *Amores perros,* Jorge's (Humberto Busto) desperate cry to Octavio (Gael García Bernal), "¿Qué hiciste cabrón?" (What have you done, son of a bitch?), are heard over an almost abstract, fast-moving shot of the white line in the middle of a road, along with the whizzing of other passing cars and the sound of excessive, as yet unidentified, panting. In this almost literally breathless beginning, Cofi, Octavio's dog, is bleeding to death in the back seat of the car while an anxious and agitated Jorge desperately tries to stop the bleeding. There is blood, a car chase, screeching tires, and aggressive language, but the worst is yet to come. At a crossroads, Octavio races through a red light and violently crashes into a car coming from the left. The scene ends with a shot of a fair-haired young woman trapped inside her vehicle, covered in blood and writhing in pain, frantically asking for help.

This opening partakes of the rhetoric of excess that characterizes much of Mexican cinema, plunging us, even if we do not know it yet, right into the middle of the film's narrative (fig. 2). After a fade, the first of three intertitles, "Octavio y Susana," takes us back to an unspecified time before the crash and inaugurates the pattern whereby *Amores perros* is divided into three segments of slightly different duration, each introduced by an intertitle with the names of the two characters around whom that particular segment of the narrative revolves. At the same time, the stories are more porous than the film's threefold division anticipates, and various types of inserts from the other stories abound in each of the segments.

The jumpy and discontinuous chase scene that opens the film becomes immediately recognizable when the white line of the road reappears fifty-four minutes later over a different sound track in its proper chronological moment within Octavio's story. As the brutal collision is about to be shown again, the screen fades to black. Now a sound bridge

Figure 2. Octavio and the rhetoric of excess
at the outset of *Amores perros*.

takes us to the set of the television program that Jorge was watching just before heading off towards Cofi's last fight at the end of the previous segment. In that program, Valeria Amaya, a famous Spanish model, had been discussing her relationship with the famous Mexican actor, Andrés Salgado (Ricardo Dalmacci). Since the first segment ends with the crash and the second one starts again with the TV program, we infer that the narrative has gone back in time, but the fade is the only formal indication of this slight jump backwards. Once outside the television studio, Andrés, Valeria's fake new boyfriend, invites her for lunch and, as they arrive at what she thinks is his new apartment, she finds out that Daniel (Álvaro Guerrero), her married lover, has just left his wife and is moving in with her. On her way to a store to get the champagne that Daniel forgot to buy for the celebration, Octavio's car violently crashes into hers. The second intertitle, "Daniel y Valeria," takes us straight into the hospital waiting room, where Daniel waits for news of Valeria's condition. The crash will be repeated once more, from a completely different perspective. Around twenty-five minutes from the end of the film, el Chivo's attentive stalking of his next victim is abruptly disrupted by the sound of colliding metal and shattering glass. He hurries to the spot and leaves shortly after with Octavio's wallet and the seriously wounded Cofi. This time there is no intertitle after the accident, since the film's third intertitle, "El Chivo y Maru," has already appeared ten minutes earlier to take us back in the film's chronological timeline to some imprecise moment previous to the crash.

Like the four repetitions of the car crash, the three intertitles structure the narrative of *Amores perros* but do not divide it into three identical and perfectly balanced parts. Each episode has its own timeline and needs to find its particular way to be told—an idiosyncrasy that is reinforced by the visual differences between them. The intertitles take us back in time in episodes one and three and slightly forward in episode two. In episodes one and two, they are prompted by the images of the car crash, but not in episode three, where the intertitle follows immediately after the ending of Valeria's story.

In each episode, there is also an uneven distribution of the events previous to and following the accident. Octavio's storyline is more concerned with the events happening before and those leading up to the accident. There are three inserts from his story in the third episode, but none in the second. Valeria and Daniel's story is mainly concerned with how the accident tragically changes their lives, even if there are also three inserts of Daniel in the first episode, and Valeria manages to make an appearance through the television set in Octavio's room. El Chivo's story is the most porous of the three, and it is more evenly distributed along the film's whole temporal arc—seven inserts in Octavio's episode and two in Valeria's. His storyline includes both his life before the accident—his discovery of his wife's death and his first incursions into his daughter's life—and how his on-the-spot decision to adopt Octavio's wounded dog will radically alter his life. The temporal structure of *Amores perros* is therefore more complex and irregular than it may seem at first sight. Yet irregularities and asymmetries are carefully balanced and contrived, emphasizing the tension between similarities and differences in the predicaments of the various inhabitants of the city. This peculiar organization of events points to the crucial role played by temporal simultaneity in the film's signifying structure and in its deployment of multiprotagonist film conventions. In the following pages we would like to focus on the consequences and reverberations of this temporal simultaneity.

Cities have become a privileged setting for a certain trend within the multiprotagonist film. The self-enclosed milieus and relatively tight groups of the early incursions into the genre—a pattern that Margrit Tröhler has called "ensemble films" on the basis of a common locale in which all characters get together at some point in the narrative—gave way to looser collections of individuals, or "mosaic films," according to Tröhler. A type of urban dynamics characterized among other things by the random intersections of absolute strangers crossing paths in all sorts of public places proved a fertile ground to explore the genre's concern with how accident and chance shape and affect human lives and human interaction. This interest in random connections can be traced back to an early example, *Grand Hotel*, with its crisscrossing of an ensemble of life-weary characters in the lobby and the corridors of its art-deco hotel. Yet, in the last decade of the twentieth century, filmic representations of contingency and the circuitous nature of human interaction acquired special relevance as a series of social and scientific discourses started to kindle the collective imagination in characteristic and unprecedented ways. David Bordwell's term for these films, "network narratives" (*Way Hollywood*), evokes such discourses, as does Wendy Everett's term, "fractal films." Everett's label suggests the ways in which chaos, small-world, and network theory have influenced the representation of urban space in films such as *Short Cuts, Magnolia, Code Unknown,* and *Intermission.* In these movies, accidental encounters of several sorts trigger unexpected connections between otherwise unrelated characters, enmeshing them into a complex network of direct and indirect relationships. These random intersections carry most of the narrative weight and may end up deflecting the plot in unexpected directions. They are not simply the means to tell a story: they are the story itself. The reverberations and patterns of similarity within difference generated through such intersections create the plot, and not vice versa. The notion of temporal simultaneity is almost always central in the articulation of these concepts into a multiprotagonist narrative, often substituting for the traditional forward-moving plot as the films' organizing principle.

The car accident in *Amores perros* is the hub of the film, the event that makes the lives of three strangers converge and collide in the streets of Mexico City (fig. 3). As in most multiprotagonist films, this intersection is a matter of pure chance and alters the lives of the characters in unpredictable ways. The traffic accident—the most common chance-based convergence in network narratives, according to Bordwell

Figure 3. Tragic crossroads: the car crash
in *Amores perros*.

(*Poetics* 204)—is also the only moment in the film in which the three stories coincide in the same space and time. Unlike other multiprotagonist films, including Iñárritu's two following movies, *Amores perros* does not forge further connections between its characters to ultimately join them together in a close net of direct and indirect relationships. The lives of Valeria, Octavio, and el Chivo clash only once; each character copes with the aftereffects in complete ignorance of the fates of the rest of the people involved. For all its visual prominence and emotional impact, the accident is just an accident, and it does not facilitate more intricate links between the narrative segments. It neither drives characters' lives together—as is the case in *21 Grams*—nor leads them to overtly reflect on the contingency and the circuitous nature of human life, as, for instance, in *Thirteen Conversations about One Thing*. The storytelling technique chosen to narrate simultaneous actions also separates *Amores perros* from other examples of the genre. Most multiprotagonist movies resort to parallel editing to move from one character or set of characters to the next without compromising spectators' ability to comprehend the narrative or the film's chronology. *Amores perros* arranges its simultaneous stories in mostly self-contained episodes and then narrates each one in sequence. A more convoluted story than it may seem at first sight and the repetition of certain events are not the only consequences of a storytelling choice that crucially affects the way spectators engage with the characters and the film's portrayal of life in an urban space.

One of the most immediate consequences of multiprotagonist storytelling patterns is frequently the way in which the spectators' implication and engagement in the movie world is influenced by the absence of a central identification point. Multiprotagonist films such as *City of Hope, Short Cuts, Magnolia,* and *Crash* force the spectator to constantly shift from one character and storyline to the next, which does not prevent identification with the characters onscreen but makes it more fragmentary, transitory, and sometimes even problematic due to the contrasting voices and perspectives articulated around them. The three self-contained episodes of *Amores perros,* however, allow us to engage with each set of characters almost as if a single story were being told, emphasizing the particular predicaments and the emotional intensity of each of the individual stories. Octavio's fratricidal rivalry with Ramiro (Marco Pérez), Valeria and Daniel's physical and emotional entrapment, and el Chivo's loss of humanity and frail regeneration are intensified by their stories being told in three self-enclosed chunks. Had the stories been narrated by means of parallel editing, the predicaments of the characters would have remained the same, but the feelings conveyed would have seemed less harrowing and excruciating. This storytelling choice also determines the almost obsessive insistence with which the movie revisits the moment of the accident in each episode and, therefore, its visual prominence. The emotional impact of the crash works through accumulation: each repetition resonates within the previous ones, increasing the violent impact of the collision and its effect on the audience.

The use of sequential narrative in *Amores perros* intensifies the emotions of each of the individual stories, but it also manages to convey temporal simultaneity in a vivid and immediate way. The four repetitions of the accident are the most obvious way of emphasizing the synchronicity of the three stories. The film does not return to the accident merely to reiterate a familiar moment but to add information and an additional perspective to the action. The first time the accident is shown, we only see two anxious young men on the run with a wounded dog in the back seat crashing into an anonymous woman. With the second repetition, we find out the reasons for their frenzied race. When the film returns to the accident for the third time, it is to tell who the fair-haired woman is and the circumstances that led her to be driving through that spot at that specific moment. The fourth replaying shows the scene from the eyes of a witness and reveals what happened to Cofi after the crash. Each time we see the event, an additional layer is added to that fateful moment, broadening our perspective on the accident and on the lives that collide at that specific time and place. The crash reverberates across different lives and stories, providing a very tangible sense of Mexico City as a place seething with a multitude of simultaneous lives and stories brimming over with fears, hopes, and desires in a constant state of friction and flow. Characters' needs, plans, and desires clash either in a direct way—as is the case of Octavio and el Jarocho (Gustavo Sánchez Parra), Octavio and Ramiro, or Gustavo (Rodrigo Murray) and Luis (Jorge Salinas)—or in more indirect ones: Octavio's desperate flight truncates Valeria and Daniel's high hopes for their new life together, and el Chivo's abject existence is shattered and transformed by his on-the-spot decision to adopt a wounded dog. In this sense, the inserts from other characters' lives that permeate each of the episodes, apart from emphasizing the temporal simultaneity of the three stories, also suggest the ease and immediacy with which, in an urban environment, almost any life and story can intrude into, interrupt, and disrupt others.

"Si quieres hacer reír a Dios, cuéntale tus planes" (If you want to make God laugh, tell him your plans) was Susana's (Vanessa Bauche) grandmother's favorite pearl of worldly wisdom—and apparently also a favorite of the director's father (Muñoz 25–26). Unlike Iñárritu's second feature, the role and place of God in relation to human life is never directly addressed in *Amores perros*. Yet, whether because of God's will or because of random chance, characters' plans and desires are continually thwarted, altered, or altogether curtailed when they, accidentally or not, clash with the plans and desires of others in the streets of Mexico City. By multiplying the number of main characters and adopting temporal simultaneity as its organizing principle, the film emphasizes the role played by fortuity and chance over cause-and-effect links and thus joins other multiprotagonist films in challenging the notion, so often championed in other genres, of an all-powerful individual whose actions can propel the world regardless of external circumstances. In *Amores perros,* broken dreams and failed plans link each character and episode to the next: from Octavio's hoped-for trip with Susana to Ciudad Juárez to

Daniel and Valeria's glamorous life together and el Chivo's revolutionary ideals. Individual agency is seriously curtailed in an urban environment whose potential for random interactions frustrates even the best-laid plans and renders risible and futile any sense of control that characters may think they have over their own destinies.

The city's endless potential for fortuitous encounters is directly evoked in those scenes in which characters or visual motifs from two different episodes are juxtaposed. In episode three, el Chivo, on his way to a photo booth, accidentally passes by Susana and Ramiro, who have not been seen or mentioned since they left the family home toward the end of episode one (fig. 4). This accidental crisscrossing, a staple of the multiprotagonist film genre, locates this specific moment in el Chivo's timeline in relation to Octavio's, thus adding to the general sense of temporal simultaneity between the stories. Even if almost an hour of filmic time has passed, the swollen eye and bruises on Ramiro's face place this encounter not very long after he has been assaulted and harshly beaten by the thugs hired by Octavio. This fortuitous and apparently irrelevant event immediately invokes the invisible presence of Octavio and reminds us that, even if his episode is over, his story is still

Figure 4. Enhancing simultaneity:
El Chivo crosses paths with Ramiro and
Susana in *Amores perros*.

very much alive. At this moment, in a different part of the city, Octavio is probably ransacking Susana's bedroom in search of the money he won with the dogfights. Through this inconsequential encounter, the film reactivates the internal point of view on Octavio's story and, at the same time, puts it into perspective within an urban context through el Chivo's eyes. While the spectator is aware of the circumstances that led Susana and Ramiro to aimlessly wander the streets of Mexico City and can almost feel some of the echoes of their story in a different part of the city—Doña Concha's (Adriana Barraza) suffering and Octavio's rage, frustration, and despair—for el Chivo, Ramiro and Susana are just a couple of passersby, no different from all the rest of the anonymous couples around him, at most a reminder of his unbearable loneliness. The device, therefore, allows us to explore the workings of spectatorial engagement in film narratives while furthering the narrative through the activation of seemingly contradictory emotional responses. The young couple's unexpected appearance in the middle of "somebody else's" episode immediately recuperates the poignancy of Octavio's feelings, the drama of Susana's married life, and the uncertain future that awaits a group of unfortunate young characters whose existence is marked by their social milieu. At the same time, that social milieu is impersonal and relentless, and these characters' circumstances are no different from those of many others. The brief reframing of the story within el Chivo's episode prompts us to disengage emotionally and look at them more clinically, as part of a much greater urban network. Through simultaneity and repetition with a difference, *Amores perros* manages to elicit both responses at the same time.

These are not the only two ways in which the film interpellates the spectator at this point. These two perspectives are also framed by an external one, represented here by the film's sound track. Celia Cruz's song "La vida es un carnaval" (Life is a carnival)—a general plea for optimism in the face of adversity (Smith, *Amores* 56)—works as an ironic commentary on the painful lives of the characters (especially of Ramiro, Susana, and Octavio at this point), but, in a more abstract sense, it also reflects the indifference of an urban context that remains impervious to and unaffected by the myriad stories, crises, and miseries haunting its streets. If the use of sequential narrative intensifies our engagement with the specific situations of the characters in each of the stories, these accidental intersections allow the simultaneous articulation of several points of view with differing degrees of engagement with each particular story. The effect of this play of perspectives is not so much one of detachment from the individual stories as an attempt to bring to life the complex mosaic of lives and voices that make up the urban environment of Mexico City. In films, as in life, it is impossible to have direct and immediate access to all incidents taking place at a specific time, but *Amores perros* attempts to convey something close to that effect by allowing us to feel the multisided complexity of life in an urban space.

The removal of the image from Valeria's last publicity campaign, later in the third episode, as a now shaved and short-haired Chivo has some pictures of his new self taken, conveys a similar effect. The huge billboard is just a piece of the urban landscape for el Chivo, who inadvertently passes it on his way to his daughter's house. Yet for Valeria and for the spectator, the Enchant advertisement tells a different story. The huge billboard with Valeria's image is first seen from Daniel's point of view from the inside of his family car as an insert of their story in the middle of the first episode. Looming over the streets of Mexico City, Valeria's sensuous and glamorous image contrasts with the confined space and the daily drags of Daniel's family life and represents a more promising future. After the accident, the privileged view of the billboard from the couple's new apartment becomes a painful reminder of the plenitude and allure of the recent past, but also a ray of hope that things may soon be back to the way they were. Later in the film, when Valeria returns home from her second visit to the hospital, she finds her image gone and the billboard for rent. The blank space in front of her window now evokes not only the transient nature of beauty, happiness, and success but also the couple's uncertain future. All these layers of meaning, created by the repetition with difference of a common motif, reverberate at this moment, making Valeria and Daniel's story as vivid and devastating as when it is narrated in episode two. At the same time, from a different perspective, we now see a couple of workers routinely removing an advertisement from a billboard whose rental period has expired (fig. 5). There will be nothing further from the minds of these two anonymous inhabitants of the city than the tragedy of the model featured in the campaign. As he drives away from it, el Chivo is similarly

Figure 5. Juggling emotional responses
from different perspectives: the poster of
Valeria in *Amores perros*.

unconcerned with Valeria's fate, of which he knows nothing, even though he is present at the moment of the car crash. The two characters' lives cross at these two moments, but they can hardly be said to impinge on one another. Rather, el Chivo undergoes his own anxious journey of rediscovery and reconciliation, an experience that is no less important than Valeria's. The spectator is empowered by the narrative to juggle both emotional responses and more, precisely because of the textual emphasis on simultaneity.

The reverberations of Valeria's image on the billboard, like the repetitions of the traffic accident, are only two examples that show the cumulative nature of the narrative and emotional structures of *Amores perros*. Similar motifs are repeated within a specific story and also move from one story to the next: from the running metaphor of dogs to the motif of absent fathers and the failed projects that permeate the three stories. As Valeria's image is being taken down from the billboard, el Chivo, now Martín, is taking the first steps toward his new life, which, at the end of the film, is still a complete mystery to him. His knowledge of his own future is as feeble as Valeria's, who will need to start anew and away from the catwalks and the fashion shoots. The scene just before el Chivo's regeneration shows Octavio, at the bus station, limping toward an unfathomable future in which the only certainty is that, even after death, Ramiro continues to emerge triumphant from their fratricidal fight. The three endings become actual beginnings for the three characters who, in spite of the different specificities of their predicaments, are now distorted reflections of one another.

In the conflict-ridden, multisided world of *Amores perros*, identity is defined not only by individual psychology but also by context and relationships. The identities of the three main characters become more complex through their reverberations and reflections on one another. It is not, as in Iñárritu's later films, that contact with the other changes people's lives in irreversible ways and turns us into new human beings, the possessors of a new identity. The car accident brings the characters together only momentarily before they go their separate ways again. Yet, the crash functions as the narrative fulcrum that allows the movie to weave its own urban network society and to link the three protagonists through parallels and construct their identities according to a new logic. In a network society, and more specifically in the Mexico City of *Amores perros*, individual identities are always inevitably contextual. Identities are created not only from what the characters do (and what they fail to accomplish) but also through their reflections in others. This feeling permeates the three stories and the three social strata depicted in the film. Identity seems to reside less in the individual and more in how the individual organizes and articulates his or her relationships with others, a view that evokes a recurrent convention of multiprotagonist films in which characters are not defined solely by their own actions but by those of other characters: similarity and difference, similarity in difference. Within this contextual view of identity, the emphasis on simultaneity instead of progression and sequentiality suggests that the search for primary causes is futile. It has sometimes been claimed that Cofi's running away from home—or Susana inadvertently letting him run away—triggers the whole chain of events (Arriaga qtd. in Scott 387), but the multisidedness of *Amores perros* does not allow for such oversimplification. Through its almost obsessive emphasis on simultaneity, the film continually exudes the feeling of the number of things that need to happen for something to take place, a point that, within the context of guilt and forgiveness, takes central stage in Iñárritu's second feature, *21 Grams*.

Where Did It All Begin?

"The Earth turned to bring us closer." This line from the Venezuelan poet Eugenio Montejo, quoted by Paul halfway through *21 Grams*, refers to the number of small things that must coincide in a time and place for something to happen. Paul is invoking the power of numbers, chaos theory, and the geometrical patterns of fractals, those complex—that is, nonlinear—systems formed on the basis of the random repetition of simple designs, and the role they play in our attempts to understand a mystery "that's bigger than us." Behind these brief observations about his job as a mathematics professor, he is also referring to his attraction to and growing affection for Cristina, but he might as well be talking about the nature of the events that make up the narrative structure of the film as a whole, from the accident that brings the characters together to Cristina's unexpected pregnancy at the end of the film. Paul's discourse and the film's constant emphasis on the randomness of experience contrast with Jack's (Benicio del Toro) tribulations about the place of human responsibility in a world in which God is ultimately responsible for every human and nonhuman action. His faith-based determinism apparently stands at the opposite pole from Paul's espousal of chaos theory.

Several critics identify a similar kind of determinism as part of the text's ideology, invoking its circular narrative structure—the film starts and ends with Paul's death—as an acknowledgment of the power of destiny and fate (Hahn 53; Cameron 73). This reading aligns critics with the director's well-known religious beliefs and allows them to explore questions of fate, causality, redemption, and faith in his second feature film. Robert Hahn's interesting review is a good illustration of this line of inquiry in its relentless search for the role played by fate in the characters' lives. Significantly, in the end Hahn finds nothing beyond the inscrutability of destiny, which may be tantamount to saying that destiny is only an expedient way of speaking about that which we do not understand, a worthy topic of tragedy, as Hahn reminds us.

Alternatively, through its use of the conventions of the multiprotagonist genre, the film provides another frame for interpretation that may be more historically and culturally specific. The complexity of human interaction and the proliferation of links between human beings are among this genre's concerns, and its use of a fragmented temporal structure suggests the contemporary feeling of a world beyond our grasp. *21 Grams*, through its very careful, coherent, and highly original construction of temporality, undermines our search for explanations. It bends, inverts, and scrambles events to underline the role of coincidence, the uselessness as well as the inevitability of looking for causes beyond random occurrences. That does not mean that the film is a random exercise aiming to reflect a random universe. The narrative structure of *21 Grams* is highly contrived, and the segments that constitute it are carefully organized, even if chronological order is subordinated to other types of continuity between the segments.

A relatively detailed description of the initial sequence will give an idea of the film's approach to the representation of time. *21 Grams* opens with a shot of a man and a woman in bed. The woman sleeps peacefully as the man, sitting next to her, gazes down and smokes a cigarette. A bright white light comes in through the window and merges with the white sheets, instilling a sense of repose and a glow only disrupted by the male character's concerned look and the almost imperceptible shaking of the handheld camera, which seems to accompany his slow breathing and deep meditations.

After the film's title—white and red letters over a black screen—a detail shot of a glass of soda and a straw transports us to the diner where two little girls and their father are eating lunch before going home. The girls are reluctant to go, but he insists, and they get ready to leave. Their movement is followed by a shot of the woman we have seen before, Cristina, at a rehabilitation therapy group meeting, describing her experiences with drugs. She remarks the crucial role that her husband and daughters—the man and the girls in the previous shot, although we do not know this yet—have played in her recovery. After that, we move to another sort of therapy. In a makeshift religious center, a born-again Christian, Jack, is lecturing a young man on the need to think twice before acting. This longer scene is followed by a shot of a flock of birds flying away at dusk, the fluttering of their wings giving way to the first musical notes in the film. The musical theme can then be heard over a detail shot of a fluorescent lightbulb, which is soon revealed to be framed from the point of view of the man in the opening shot, Paul. He is now in intensive care, his pale body swollen with tubes and needles. In voiceover he starts mulling over the frailty of the boundary that separates life and death. A bare lightbulb then takes us to a squalid bathroom where Cristina, in a black top, is snorting cocaine in front of a mirror. Miles away from the self-confident, balanced, and grateful woman at the rehabilitation therapy, she now looks distressed and disturbed, displaced to the edge of the frame, shown from a high angle and suffused in a yellowish light.

From the medium close-up of Cristina, the film cuts to an extreme close-up of Paul's wife, Mary (Charlotte Gainsbourg), in a much paler light but with a similar look of anguish, reinforced by the tight frame, in her visit to a gynecologist. As we learn of her fallopian-tube damage and her ardent desire to have a baby, we also find out that her husband is dying. There is a brief follow-up to the scene between Jack and the young man, which, after a violent argument, ends with Jack driving home to his family. The sequence concludes with five brief shots of Paul, sitting by a derelict swimming pool with a gun in his hands, overcome by impotence and desperation. This feeling of desolation filters through into the next segment, which follows Jack along a prison corridor and into a cell.

The segment that has just been described lasts approximately nine minutes. In it, the main characters and strands of the film's multiprotagonist plot are introduced, but not in chronological order. The three different glimpses of Cristina's and Paul's lives do not hold if we read them sequentially. Jack's narrative line is chronological at the beginning, but when we see him being locked up in jail, the time lapse—be it backward or forward in the timeline of the story—becomes evident. In fact, the events depicted in this initial sequence take place at different moments over the course of several months. However, the film does not provide us with any temporal clues to help locate them in an accurate timeline, a complete understanding of which can only be grasped once the film is over. Even then, although events can be identified as previous or subsequent to other events, there is never a full understanding of their overall ordering. For example, we know that Cristina's group therapy and Mary's visit to the doctor are previous to the accident, but it is as impossible as it is irrelevant to look for the temporal relation between those two actions. Unlike *Amores perros*, simultaneity is not the point. Apart from the moments in which individual lives collide, the film is not interested in highlighting temporal relations between events happening in different narrative lines.

If *Amores perros* is obsessed with simultaneous lives and actions to show the multisidedness, complexity, and contradictions of life in an urban space, *21 Grams* aims to transcend physical time (and, in a sense, physical space) and links characters and storylines through their feelings and emotions. The accident, so visually prominent in *Amores perros*, remains offscreen. The actual collision is never seen, but, due to the film's scrambled structure, it can be painfully felt from the beginning to the end of the narrative.

In this first sequence, Jack's scenes at the religious center are the longest and the only ones that follow one another chronologically. But lack of chronological continuity between contiguous scenes implies neither disorder nor arbitrariness, and alternative organizing patterns emerge behind the film's disregard for linear storytelling. In the absence of a main character, a clear cause-and-effect chain, or chronological cues to locate the scenes in a temporal framework, what holds these brief and achronological snatches together is the emotional continuum that emerges from the juxtaposition of textures and feelings, creating unexpected links between the various characters. The visual and emotional qualities of these brief moments merge from one scene to the next and are intensified through the patterns of similarity and contrast that spread through the whole film, joining scenes, characters, and narrative lines regardless of the narrative or temporal context. In the sequence described above, the desolation evoked by the sight of Paul in intensive care blends into Cristina's inner chaos and isolation in her solo scene and is in turn transferred to Mary's anguish and desperation during her visit to the doctor. Regardless of the characters' specific predicaments and the chronological sequence, the intensity of each scene adds to the next, and the result is always bigger than the sum of the parts. In *21 Grams*, chronological time, if never completely abandoned, loses much of its momentum in favor of emotional time, as Iñárritu has often remarked (in Romney, "Emotional" 15).

The film does not seem as interested in showing what happens next or what the consequences or causes of a specific event may be as in creating an emotional web in which feelings are not restricted to a specific cause or moment in time but rather permeate the narrative from beginning to end. In the sequence described above, two adjoining scenes link Cristina and Jack in their self-confidence and satisfaction at having left behind a turbulent past, an experience that both of them are now using to help others. Some scenes later, as we see Cristina sniffing cocaine and Jack entering a prison cell, they are linked again through the sharp turns that, for reasons still unknown to us, both their lives seem to have taken. Since at this point we still do not know which moment comes first in each character's life, we can only surmise that life is a succession of ups and downs, and neither chronology nor causality constitutes its main driving force. As the film develops and the accident tragically links their lives together, the emotional continuities between these two characters also proliferate. In the scene described at the beginning of this book, for instance, Cristina, alone in her bedroom, tortures herself by listening to her husband's voice message once and again. The sequence ends with a long shot of her lying in bed, overcome by impotence and grief. A straight cut then takes us to a scene in which Jack, alone in the motel, is burning out the last traces of his religious past from his tattooed forearms and pouring alcohol into his open wounds. The sad tango music playing over both scenes unifies and intensifies both characters' desperation, suffering, and self-inflicted torture. A close-up of Jack's face leaning forward to the left as he watches his flesh sizzle with alcohol cuts to one of Cristina leaning over a table, facing right, snorting cocaine (figs. 6–7). The inverted graphic match shows Jack and Cristina as almost mirror images of each other—their heads semireclined in extreme close-up, their eyes lowered, their expressions revealing extreme anguish—and unites them through their suffering and their tendency toward self-destruction as the only way to soothe the pain and go on living. Not only do these formal connections suggest parallels and contrasts between people's feelings; more intangibly, they suggest the existence of ineffable currents constantly running between us, joining us together with others even if we never become aware of it. Through these reverberations, the film emphasizes and amplifies characters' emotions but also suggests that, no matter how painfully isolated people appear to be in Iñárritu's fictional world, they are ultimately deeply connected: our passions are revealed to be part of a complex web, which is precisely what makes us human.

Connections of this kind are not restricted to Cristina and Jack,

Figures 6–7. Invisible currents:
Jack and Cristina in *21 Grams*.

the two characters most directly affected by the accident. Rather, the
film bends and distorts chronology, enmeshing all the characters and
storylines in a common space in which a character's feelings resonate
within and are magnified by their reverberations on others. Let us look
at another example in some detail. A shot of a balloon in the now silent
and empty room where Jack's birthday party was going to take place
opens the scene in which Jack finds out that the people he ran over
are now dead, and he decides to turn himself in. His wife, Marianne

(Melissa Leo), desperately tries to stop him, but he reminds her of his moral responsibility to the victims and leaves. A nervous close-up of Marianne's despair at seeing her family crumble to pieces the night of the accident is linked by means of a straight cut with a scene in which Cristina, sometime after that fateful night, painfully puts her children's toys away in the garage.

The musical theme that joins the two women in their suffering reinforces the continuum that allows Marianne's feelings to flow into Cristina's, in spite of the differences between the situations they are going through. By means of this strategy, the film prompts comparisons between the traumatic perspective of a woman who has unexpectedly lost her children and that of one whose children's future is uncertain because of their father's erratic behavior. The successive presentation of the two moments underlines their narrative and thematic interdependence: the future of Marianne's children is indelibly joined to the deaths of Cristina's, while Marianne's legitimate yet temporary worry is reframed within Cristina's much more definitive despair. As Cristina goes upstairs, she stops in front of her daughters' bedroom, opens the door slightly, and looks in. A point-of-view shot of the space that her daughters used to occupy with the blurred frame of the bedroom door in the foreground captures her misery and the unbearable void that she feels all around her. Still unable to enter the room, she closes the door and leans her head against it. The cardboard hearts that decorate the door match the heart-shaped chocolate cake that opens the following scene in which Paul and Mary celebrate the success of Paul's heart transplant with a group of friends. The laughter and jokes coming from Paul's welcome-home party do not only mark an abrupt change from the melancholy musical notes linking Marianne and Cristina but also recall the celebration, Jack's birthday party, that never took place, and which indirectly made Paul's celebration possible.

The continuum that structures these three scenes does not stop at the contrast between the two sets of characters and the direct consequences of the accident for both groups—loss for Jack, Marianne, and Cristina and gain for Mary and Paul. A sequence of shots of Paul toasting to the beginning of his new life ends with a shot of the whole group doubly framed by the threshold of the door. The framing of this shot is almost identical to Cristina's earlier point-of-view shot of her daughters' bedroom, even if that of the dinner party is not mediated by a character's subjective perspective, and the frame of the door remains in sharp focus (figs. 8–9). The parallels and connections between the two shots are obvious. The packed and lively frame of Paul and Mary's dining room is not only a direct consequence of the void in Cristina's daughters' room, but the impending role that Cristina will play in Paul's new life can be acutely felt through the choice of a similar framing strategy. Cristina can almost be seen on the other side of that door, and her present misery impreg-

Figures 8–9. Framing anticipates intimacy
between Paul and Cristina in *21 Grams*.

nates the tone of the celebration, which does not feel as optimistic as it had a few seconds earlier while the camera remained inside the room, a feeling emphasized by the double framing, the wide-angle, and the distance of the camera. Conversely, it could be argued that the second shot fills the emptiness of the first one: the emotional space formerly occupied by Michael and the children in Cristina's heart will soon be partly filled by Paul and, further along in the story, by the new baby that will be the result of her brief but intense relationship with him. Thus the respectively empty and packed frames feed off each other, jump across chronological times, and underline human relatedness, even in stories like that narrated by 21 Grams, in which the characters often ache with loneliness and alienation. Although in the story Paul and Cristina's lives have not crossed yet, their imminent relationship can already be strongly felt through this framing strategy, Cristina metaphorically looking on from outside the party room, Paul hovering over the empty desk of the children.

As the camera goes inside the dining room again, Mary's public announcement of her (and supposedly also Paul's) decision to become parents is met with an unenthusiastic and even hostile reaction from her husband. Paul's new life does not seem to include Mary, and a series of shot/reverse shots shows the growing estrangement and awkward-ness between the couple. The scene finishes with a close-up of Mary that emphasizes her fragility but also her determination to hold on to her idea of a family that she knows is quickly disintegrating in front of her. Although the connection is not visually emphasized in this case, the similarity between the framings may also prompt the spectator to compare the feelings of the two women: while Cristina's children have tragically disappeared, Mary's are only a distant dream. In a film that, like the other two Iñárritu films analyzed in this book, is very much about parents and children, the links between the two mothers proliferate, especially when we find out, toward the end of the narrative, that both women are going to have babies by the same father.

In accordance with the film's emotional rather than chronological logic, Mary's close-up is followed not by the aftermath of the celebra-tion—a scene that the film resumes three scenes later—but by a brief scene, presumably later in the film's chronological timeline, that shows Paul's first meeting with the private investigator he hires to find out the identity of the donor. As was the case with the links mentioned above, this jump forward is neither capricious nor random. This brief scene, which literally interrupts the celebration right after Mary's announcement, does not only reveal how different Paul's and Mary's plans for the future are; it also puts an abrupt end to Paul's cheerful and optimistic attitude toward his new life. By means of this and other temporal dislocations, the film does not allow events to run their proper chronological course but rather constantly interrupts them with glimpses from the future that announce and underline the evanescent nature of these moments of happiness. Even before the actual celebration is over, we already know that Paul's present feeling of victory over death will soon shudder and crumble under his desire to find his new self.

The way in which the film scrambles and bends time makes time lapses like these a constant in *21 Grams*. When a peaceful walk back to Cristina's place after lunch ends with her inviting Paul in for a drink, the film unexpectedly cuts to an establishing shot of the derelict motel where Cristina's desire for revenge will later take them (figs. 10–11). Inside the motel, we are shown a shot of Cristina asleep and Paul, in the background, sitting up, visibly anxious and distressed but determined to go out and kill Jack to revenge the death of Cristina's family. The peace and serenity felt at the restaurant and on the walk back have been replaced by distress, agony, and revenge. The way in which space is constructed in these shots also contributes crucially to the complex emotions that the text asks the spectator to share at this point, but in purely temporal terms, we are confronted with the cruel and abrupt way in which Cristina and Paul's happiness has been cut short by a snatch of their future, which highlights the ephemerality of the present and the need to treasure it while it lasts. As Paul tells Cristina over lunch, the chances of two people getting together are minimal, and, as the film continually reminds us by means of temporal lapses like those mentioned here, when such meetings happen, they have already started to disappear. In the film's achronological arrangement of events, the mutual attraction between Paul and Cristina leads to chaos, misery, and death even before any kind of intimacy is allowed to develop between them. Thus, the rare moments of intimacy and stability are always undermined by a sense of fragility and loss. Happiness, serenity, and communication are indeed possible in *21 Grams*, but, as a result of the film's scrambled chronology,

Figures 10–11. Emotional time: from happiness
to desolation in only one cut in *21 Grams*.

they can only take place in the interstices of time and are surrounded
by an intense awareness of their fleetingness and evanescence.

As Jonathan Romney has argued, the interruptions and disruptions
of the chronological flow of *21 Grams* constitute a blunt acknowledgment of the instability and precariousness of human life and identity
("Enigma" 16). Due to the film's scrambled narrative pattern, it is impossible to speak with any accuracy about a time before and a time after the
accident. Rather, the accident, an indication of how futile and fragile any

human attempt at stability and permanence can ever be, permeates the whole film, from its very first shot to the last. Its presence is a constant in the way it affects characters and in the way the film obsessively revisits the moments previous to it several times and scatters them throughout the narrative to show its imminence and its inevitability. We see Michael leaving his voice message on Cristina's phone on the way back home. Some scenes later, it is Jack saying goodbye to his friend Brown and heading toward his birthday party. At another point it is Michael and the girls, again, this time talking briefly to the gardener and disappearing offscreen, followed by a passing truck. Then, to the sound of some screeching tires, the gardener hurries offscreen in the same direction as Michael and the girls. This is the closest we get to the accident, since the actual collision is never shown. Unlike the visual impact and the visceral quality of the crash in *Amores perros,* the looming but invisible accident in *21 Grams* floats in the air, which makes its presence more pervasive. Death in this movie is literally around every corner. Each change of scene can lead us back to the moment of the accident from a different perspective, but always with a similar result: no explanations are offered, there are no logical causes, and there is nobody to blame. The accident simply represents the sense of mortality that is intrinsic to life itself.

The film's awareness of death and of the precariousness of human existence is not necessarily as pessimistic as it may seem from the above account. Mortality, accidents, and chance are inherent to life, but so are hope, resilience, and our enormous potential to reach out to others, as the film also shows. If the scrambled narrative structure of *21 Grams* constantly curtails characters' hopes, expectations, and plans for the future, its multiprotagonist narrative structure posits human interaction and accidental connections as an environment in which hope can also be found. Near the chronological and filmic end of *21 Grams,* Cristina, who has just found out about her unexpected pregnancy, is looking out through a barred window at the snow falling over the barren field outside the hospital. Jack comes to stand near her and looks at her in silence. Cristina's equally silent look, brimming over with understanding and forgiveness in spite of the present despair, finally appeases Jack's excruciating guilt and allows him to go back to his family, at peace with himself. In that brief exchange, she also sees her own misery reflected in Jack's eyes and is able to find there the peace she needs to go on living. The redemptive quality of this brief encounter is believable and extremely moving because of the deep and intricate connections that the film's logic has previously weaved between the characters. These links crystallize at this moment of mutual understanding in which both characters can see themselves through and in the eyes of the other. This is also the sense of the three moments of past happiness that the text also includes in this final segment: Jack saying goodbye to his friend before he gets into his truck; Cristina's sister making a rude but, in this context, loving gesture to her as they get out of the swimming-pool; and Michael and Cristina's children happily and noisily leaving the restaurant. Affection and communication with those around us can be found in every little gesture, in every unexpected encounter, and although they never last, they have a way of always returning. The film's scrambled chronology links characters in their common humanity, and the intensity of that bond, the film claims, though not powerful enough to overcome death, gives us the strength to go on living. Thus, by manipulating chronological time in such an ostentatious way, the text not only emphasizes contingency and mortality but also puts forward its unbreakable faith in the power of human relationships and the resilience of human beings in their search for happiness and harmony even in the direst of circumstances. Time in 21 Grams is scrambled chronologically to construct a community of feelings and deep bonding out of the shreds and scraps of its demolished edifice.

Amores perros and 21 Grams, like other contemporary multiprotagonist films, use the narrative motif of a car accident as the core of their temporal structure, but to very different ends. In keeping with the reach and ambition of the urban canvas attempted in the former and the inwardness and basic features of common humanity sought in the latter, the crash weaves different types of networks between the characters. In Amores perros it underlines the simultaneity of three stories and suggests, through the centrality of that temporal concept, the links between a thousand more, positing the complexities and parallels of contemporary urban experience. In 21 Grams, its narrative role is more limited and more ambitious: through its peculiar and obsessive repetitiveness, it destabilizes time and brings to the fore an alternative way of structuring human experience. Thus, both narrative structures underscore the importance of temporality in Iñárritu's oeuvre. In them, time expands and contracts, becomes distorted and repeats itself ad infinitum, moves around in circles and branches off in unexpected directions—constituting, in sum, a powerful symptom of the ways in which contemporary experience has been shaped by economic, cultural, and technological phenomena. *Babel* does not abandon these preoccupations but frames them within a more ambitious, worldwide canvas, linking the film to recent theoretical speculations about the human comprehension of time in the face of contemporary globalizing phenomena. For this reason, we devote the next section to the exploration of various reverberations of the temporal structure of the film, with particular attention to its ending.

Forever Now

When, toward the end of *Babel,* Susan (Kate Blanchett) arrives safely at the hospital in Casablanca and Richard (Brad Pitt) rings home to speak to Amelia (Adriana Barraza) and his children, we realize that the film's temporal structure has not been as straightforward as we may have initially thought (fig. 12). Richard's phone call brings us back to an earlier moment in the film's timeline, some hours before Amelia's fateful decision to take Mike (Nathan Gamble) and Debbie (Elle Fanning) with

Figure 12. Temporal manipulations:
Richard telephones home in *Babel.*

her to her son's wedding in Mexico. At this point in the movie, though, we already know what the consequences of Amelia's action are going to be. On their way back from the wedding, the car driven by Amelia's nephew, Santiago (Gael García Bernal), is stopped at a border control and, after a tense confrontation with the officer, Santiago races through the checkpoint and later continues his escape on his own, leaving Amelia and the kids stranded in the middle of the desert. All this has already been seen when we witness Richard's call, even though chronologically it has not happened yet.

Like Iñárritu's previous films, *Babel* manipulates time to tell several stories linked by a tragic event—not a traffic accident in this case but the accidental shooting of a tourist in Morocco. The temporal structure of *Babel* and its effects are also different from its predecessors. While Iñárritu's first feature film tells three simultaneous stories in sequence, *Babel* crosscuts between four stories taking place at different moments over a five-day span. This storytelling choice cancels out the chronological sequence between the stories and provides them with an appearance of simultaneity that later evaporates with Richard's telephone call. There are other, less obvious indications of the temporal dislocations between the stories—twice in the Tokyo segment, TV news programs refer to the incident in Morocco, revealing to the attentive spectator that this story is taking place a few days later than the rest—but the repetition of Richard's telephone call, this time within his and Susan's storyline, finally gives the temporal structure of the film away: while the two stories that take place in Morocco are roughly simultaneous (or at least start at approximately the same moment), Amelia's sets out right after Richard's phone call, whereas Chieko's (Rinko Kikuchi) happens a few days later.

The film's constant mixture of tenses urges us to speculate about the relativity and flexibility of time, a feature that *Babel* shares with other multiprotagonist movies. These films complicate linear time almost by definition, the proliferation of stories demanding different timelines and the coexistence and commensurability of events of diverse durations, questioning the validity of the notion of the closed ending as the culmination of the linear narrative. The worldwide dimension of the narrative space in *Babel,* to which we return in the final section of this book, determines the textual treatment of time and increases its mal-

leability. As in the two previous films, time is cut down to the size of individual and interpersonal human experience, but in its articulation within a story about the effects of globalization and transnationalism, it reverberates with connotations of the complex nature of contemporary societies. In this sense, Manuel Castells's notion of timeless time as one of the main features of the renewed social order that he calls "the network society" can be used as a starting point for the analysis of the temporal structure articulated in *Babel*.

The emergence of timeless time is for Castells a direct consequence of the ways in which the information-technology revolution of the last quarter of the twentieth century has transformed some of the fundamental dimensions of human life. Previous conceptions of time as linear, irreversible, measurable, and predictable have been shattered in a new social order that is characterized, among other things, by multiple and immediate access to almost any event happening in any part of the world. The ability to witness and maybe even take part in a series of "heres and nows" posits a serious challenge to the traditional chronological paradigm. The reign of immediacy in today's network society drastically compresses the temporal sequence, which all but disappears. Past, present, and future merge into each other and collapse into an eternal now, a feature that, especially in the undifferentiated temporal collages created by the media, is becoming a "decisive feature of our culture, shaping the minds and memories of children educated in the new cultural context" (492). Castells describes timeless time as both eternal and ephemeral: eternal because it is forever anchored in the here and now, and ephemeral because each temporal arrangement is constantly rewritten by the context. Timeless time, therefore, is characteristic of our society, but it is not the only temporality available nowadays. It coexists with another paradigm, still time-bound, since not everybody can escape the tyranny of chronological time. Castells sees the coexistence of these temporalities as the cause of one of the multiple fractures of the contemporary world: while certain privileged individuals and groups are able to transcend temporal constraints and navigate through life as in an eternal present, others still suffer the discipline and the constraints of a more traditional experience of time (492–97).

The temporal structure of *Babel* captures the dichotomy that Castells sees at the center of the network society. By crosscutting between the different temporal frameworks of four nonsimultaneous stories, the film problematizes the chronological sequentiality between them, replacing it with a falsely synchronous structure. The first transition between narrative blocks takes spectators from the remote spot in the Atlas mountains where the brothers Yussef (Boubker Ait El Caid) and Ahmed (Said Tarchani) have just shot a tourist bus to a suburban home in San Diego. Nothing in the narrative indicates that the phone conversation with which the second block starts takes place almost one day later—after Susan and Richard's nerve-wracking stay in Tazarine and their helicopter evacuation to Casablanca. Similarly, when Santiago starts the car to cross over to Mexico—to the retrospectively ominous lines from a song from the radio, "para que regreses, para que te quedes conmigo" (So that you return, so that you stay with me)—and the following block starts with several shots of a group of tourists in Morocco, including Richard and Susan having lunch in a humble restaurant in the desert, there are no indications that the film has just moved backward chronologically. Yet the feeling conveyed by these temporal shifts is not one of narrative disorientation, as was the case in *21 Grams,* since each storyline in *Babel* is told in a strictly chronological manner.

The transitions between the narrative blocks in *Babel* articulate a specific type of space, but, in terms of time, they join different temporalities in an undifferentiated present in which, to the eyes of the spectator, everything is happening at the same time. Through this temporal strategy, the film highlights the links and the sense of immediacy between events happening in distant places, thus echoing some of the social and scientific discourses that took center stage with the rise of the network society. Turning Edward Lorenz's well-known concept of the butterfly effect into one of its main tenets, the film shows how on-the-spot decisions, lapses of judgment, and small flaws can quickly snowball to unforeseeable and unintended consequences on the other side of the world, and traditional time ceases to be a relevant consideration. The shot of a rifle in Morocco can almost immediately be heard in the United States, where, on an institutional level, it soon resonates with the threat of a terrorist attack, and on a more individual level, it affects a Mexican nanny who finds herself unable to attend her son's wedding. It can also be heard in Japan, where investigations are directed to finding out whether the weapon used in the shooting came from the black market. If *Amores perros* uses the conventions of the multiprotagonist film to weave a story about simultaneous lives in an urban megalopolis, *Babel* goes a step further and extends them to a global level. *Babel* is not interested in simultaneity but in the networked nature of human life; therefore, the film crosscuts between the stories regardless of their chronology to emphasize the links between them. Had the stories been narrated in chronological order, the feeling of an intricate worldwide tapestry would not have been as powerful. As a result of its scrambled narrative, distant places and distinct temporalities are welded to tell a multiprotagonist tale about huge divisions and close connections among human beings across the globe.

In this way, the narrative structure of *Babel* seamlessly embodies Castells's notion of timeless time. Yet the film is not oblivious to the other temporal paradigm that in spite of its apparent limitations and inadequacies in today's globalized world is still present and governs the lives of millions of people. The immediacy that characterizes timeless time rules the transitions between the blocks and the other links between them, but not the individual stories. After Susan has been shot, Richard's anger, aggression, and frustration stem precisely from his being forced to cope with the constraints posed by what could be described as "Moroccan time." The slowed-down rhythms of life that he was looking for in a foreign land as a way to overcome his marital and personal crises suddenly become limitations and obstacles. The nearest hospital is three hours away, the clinic one hour and a half, and the tour guide's village, Tazarine, is not to his eyes the epitome of efficiency and expedience. The only available doctor, a vet, can only sew the open wound to stop the bleeding, and the U.S. bureaucracy complicates and slows things down even more.

Time-bound Tazarine embodies some of the temporal paradoxes of globalization. While from some places the other side of the world can be reached in a matter of hours, in other places, even the nearest hospital becomes a forbidding trip. Time in Tazarine stops and becomes unbearable not only for Richard, whose wife is seriously wounded and bleeding to death, but also for his fellow travelers, for whom suddenly the local dwellers have lost all traces of exoticism and have become menacing others. The colorful local peddlers and picturesque sights of the scene previous to the shooting are, to the tourists' eyes, nowhere to be seen in

Tazarine. Attractive exoticism has suddenly mutated into a synonym of potential Islamic terrorism, and news items, like thirty German tourists' throats having been recently slit in an Egyptian town, come to the fore and turn the curiosity to discover the other into a nightmare.

Babel is equally attuned to both ways of understanding temporality, which makes its approach to time complex and representative of the network society. The clash between these two temporal paradigms gives the film its particular structural flavor. Traditional time reigns supreme within the individual stories and within each of the blocks (six for each of the stories) that make up their narrative arcs. Each story is narrated in strict chronological order (there is only one brief although powerful flashback, clearly signaled as such, in the final block of the Moroccan brothers' story). Furthermore, the duration of the individual stories is in all cases relatively limited—probably not even two days in the longest one of them. This strict temporal arrangement, which, unlike in most films, downplays the role of ellipses, calls our attention to the materiality and density of time. Time moves at an unbearably slow pace for Richard, his fellow travelers, and even for the spectator in the Tazarine story. The wedding party in Tijuana and the stretch of time during which Amelia and the children are lost in the Sonoran desert seem never-ending. Chieko moves from the volleyball court to lunch with friends, to the dental clinic, to her house, to the square where she meets other youngsters, to the disco, and back to her house, all in a few hours, giving the impression that her day will never end. Something similar happens to Ahmed and Yussef. Particularly from the moment they find out about the consequences of their game, time for them slows down almost to a halt, their extreme worry and anxiety bringing them to a state of paralysis. For these characters, chronological time is not only real and tangible but also a central feature in their lives. At the same time, the multiprotagonist structure, in combination with the temporal arrangement of the individual stories and especially the transitions between blocks, intimates a pervading sense of immediacy and temporal dislocation.

Multiprotagonist films that, like *Babel*, narrate their stories in parallel distort temporality almost by definition, since even those that follow a strictly linear chronology have to cope with the interruptions in the narrative flow brought about by the constant shifts between sets of characters and/or storylines. Most of them turn these fractures into temporal ellipses and so, when a specific story is resumed, we assume that some time has elapsed and do not expect to find the characters in the same position or situation in which we left them. *Babel* tends to resume each narrative thread from almost its stopping point in the previous narrative block, essentially freezing the action at the transitions. At the end of the first of the twenty-four narrative blocks that make up *Babel,* the two Moroccan brothers realize that the bus they have just shot at has stopped, and they start running downhill. When the film resumes their storyline in the fifth block, an aerial shot shows a continuation of the same action: the brothers are still running away from the site. Even if almost eighteen minutes of filmic time have passed, in narrative terms practically no time has elapsed. The strategy, which is repeated in between most narrative blocks, drastically slows down the narrative progression of each of the storylines. At the end of the third block, Richard realizes that Susan is bleeding and starts asking for help. Three blocks and sixteen minutes of filmic time later, he is still asking for help and trying to lay Susan flat on the floor of the bus. Were it not for the three narrative blocks in between the shot that ends block three and the one that opens block seven, the action would look continuous. Near the end of the film, Kenji (Satoshi Nikaido), the detective investigating the provenance of the rifle with which Susan was shot, leaves Chieko's apartment with her handwritten note in his pocket. When this narrative thread is resumed in the final block of the film, he is still in the elevator, going down, and he comes across Yasujiro (Kôji Yakusho), Chieko's father, in the lobby. Again, almost ten minutes of filmic time amount to practically no chronological time at all.

In retrospect, the actual temporal span of each of the stories seems surprisingly short in relation to the filmic time used to narrate them and the intensity with which each of the stories engages the spectators. While this relative brevity results in a keen sense of the materiality and centrality of linear time in the characters' lives, their combination in a multiprotagonist structure paradoxically produces the opposite effect: as a consequence of the retardation of narrative development brought about by the temporal pauses in the transitions between blocks, time stretches and expands in such a way that we lose sense of it almost completely. The temporal development of each story becomes so slow that time dissolves and almost disappears. Time becomes malleable, flexible, and its extraordinary density within the individual stories ends up compromising its linearity. The dissolution of time in each of the storylines, combined with the merging of different chronological moments provided by the temporal shifts between blocks, creates an undifferentiated present where chronology is rendered irrelevant since, as in the case of *21 Grams,* it is the emotions and the connections between characters and storylines that come to the fore. *Babel* annuls chronological time to construct meanings about the network society and a world dominated by globalizing forces. Linearity is not abandoned, as was the case in *21 Grams,* but it is both emphasized and compromised, a strategy that resonates with the coexistence noted by Castells between chronological and timeless time in modern societies and that also influences the complex and extremely affecting final part of the film.

Bibo No Aozora

The ending of *Babel* must be seen within the context of the conventions of the multiprotagonist film. The particular sense of closure articulated in these movies is the consequence of a narrative structure that does not always move from one event to the next but branches off in different directions and concerns a variety of characters, bringing to the fore the links and connections between several strands of the plot. The well-knit and tidy resolutions that usually accompany goal-oriented single or dual protagonists who have to overcome specific obstacles or meet almost impossible deadlines are replaced in the multiprotagonist genre by a preference for open endings where unresolved conflicts and loose ends abound and narrative lines stop rather than end. Endings in the multiprotagonist genre tend to fall into Richard Neupert's category of openstory films—those movies that acknowledge that, while this particular stage of the tale is finished, there are no easy and clear-cut resolutions (102). As a specific type of open ending, multiprotagonist movies may highlight the persistence of the conflicts by going back to the beginning in a circular narrative. For example, two automobile crashes frame the narrative of *Crash,* a film where racial prejudice is portrayed as far too intricate and manifold a topic to allow oversimplification to a single cause. A similar feeling of history repeating itself emerges from *Fast Food Nation,* a multiprotagonist cross-section of the fast-food industry that features the same coyote leading two different groups of Mexicans across the desert at the beginning and the end of the narrative. None of these films takes the circular structure to the extreme of *Before the Rain*, a multiprotagonist Macedonian movie about the Balkans conflict that arranges a story told in three episodes into a perfect circle at the expense of narrative and chronological coherence and plausibility. This plot arrangement portrays deep-rooted and ancestral enmities between close neighbors in a part of the former Yugoslavia as insoluble because of their never-ending nature, but also as something that, like the structure of the film itself, defies comprehension since crucial rational leaps are necessary to perpetuate the unbroken chain of conflicts.

Iñárritu, who found the Macedonian film inspirational, adapts the specific attitude toward closure of the multiprotagonist genre, including the concept of circularity, to his own themes and concerns. From the endings of the three stories that make up *Amores perros* emerges a feeling of uncertainty that turns these endings into doors opening to an unfathomable future. Rather than as the resolution of conflicts, they are perceived as new beginnings for each of the characters. Paul's death at the end of *21 Grams* could be seen as a closed ending and therefore as a diversion from the inconclusiveness that characterizes the multiprotagonist genre. Yet that feeling of closure is counterpointed by the scrambled narrative and the unknown paths that open up for Cristina and Jack at the end. Not surprisingly, the film ends with snow falling on the motel's empty and derelict swimming pool, a powerful image of regeneration and hope and of life reemerging from even the direst circumstances. The narrative structure of *Babel* is not circular, even if Richard's phone call near the end confers upon it a touch of circularity that emphasizes the connections between the stories and reveals their chronological arrangement. The feeling in this case is not so much one of history repeating itself as of putting each of the stories into a wider perspective, a key feature in *Babel* that takes center stage as the narrative nears its end.

As with the repetitions of the car crash in *Amores perros*, the telephone conversation forces us to recontextualize the beginning of Amelia's story, now taking into consideration Richard's point of view as well. The concerned but calm voice coming from the telephone before is now revealed as that of a grief-stricken and vulnerable parent who is doing his best to hide his suffering from his son. Having access to Richard's point of view at this specific moment does not justify the way he treats Amelia when he calls again some hours later, but it provides a context for his rage and desperation when he forbids her to attend her son's wedding in Mexico. Similarly, Amelia's decision to take Mike and Debbie with her across the border may seem ill-advised and foolish—particularly given her situation as an undocumented immigrant—but it turns out to be her only option. After all, were it not for the legal restrictions, a trip across the border should not be problematic at all, since she is neither putting the children at risk nor neglecting them. Both in Mexico and in San Diego, Amelia takes care of Mike and Debbie with devotion and affection. Yet, looked at from a different angle, her decision may seem highly questionable. The film, therefore, is keen to make us share alternative perspectives on a single event, decision, or predicament. Different characters have different points of view within their own specific cultural and personal contexts, and even though those points of view may differ drastically, the text asks us to understand all of them.

This deployment of a multiplicity of perspectives also has a different but related function: it simultaneously approximates us to and distances us from specific situations and characters. The faces of Yussef and Abdullah are shown on a television set in Japan to the complete indifference of Chieko, who is surfing channels to pass the time. While the spectators are vividly aware of the tragedy of the Moroccan family behind those mug shots, they are no more than two anonymous faces from a faraway land for the Japanese girl, who is suffering from her own problems—her inability to communicate, the death of her mother, her estrangement from her father, and who knows what else (since we never find out what she writes in her note to the detective). An even more complex game of perspectives is articulated in the final narrative block when the outcome of Richard and Susan's story is reported on a news program in Japan in the last words spoken in the film: "The American people finally have a happy ending after five days of frantic phone calls and hand-wringing." As the newsreader makes clear, it is definitely a happy ending for the American family but not for the Moroccan one, who are absent from the report even though they were involved in the incident in an equally accidental manner and with even more tragic consequences. Yet, for the police detective watching this bulletin, the outcome of Susan and Richard's story is not nearly as interesting as the contents of Chieko's note; and like Chieko, he remains ignorant of the other ramifications of the Moroccan plot. *Babel* forces us to detach ourselves from an individual's micronarrative and to look at it as part of a wider ensemble of other characters, voices, and points of view. Through its complex articulation of both a chronological and a timeless temporal paradigm, our engagement with an individual and his or her suffering or happiness is put into a wider perspective when we look at it in the context of other stories of equal narrative importance. Individual stories, no matter how poignant the predicament of the protagonists or how potentially melodramatic their suffering or their happiness, look drastically different when seen from a distance. In an apparently paradoxical move, *Babel,* like other multiprotagonist movies, focuses intensely on individuals and contextualizes their experiences within a much larger canvas that underscores their insignificance.

Not only does this play of perspectives gather momentum in the final part of the movie, it is emphasized and replicated by the structure and content of the final four segments, which narrate the endings of each of the individual stories and constitute the film's finale. Slightly disrupting what until then had been the strict order of the narrative blocks, a shot of Kenji leaving Chieko's apartment is followed by a detail shot of Amelia's hands at the border-patrol station. There, she is told that Mike and Debbie have been found alive, but she is denied any additional information either on them or on her nephew, Santiago, whose fate remains one of the film's loose ends. Her story finishes with a close-up of the embrace between her and her son back in Tijuana, after she has been forced to accept voluntary deportation. Overcome by impotence and desperation, she holds on to Luis (Robert Esquivel) tightly, trying to comprehend how sixteen years of her life can be fitted into a small plastic bag. There is some dramatic irony in the fact that the next meeting between mother and son after the wedding takes place only a few hours later, in Mexico rather than the United States, where he had been planning to move if things did not work out for him and his wife in Tijuana. Sixteen years may seem a long time, but life must be taken from one day to the next for the undocumented immigrant. Security and stability are always spurious notions, and any plans for the future, as a character says in *Amores perros,* are only one more reason to make God laugh. All of a sudden, because of what looked like a harmless and apparently inconsequential decision, Amelia's life in San Diego has vanished into thin air. Her sense of identity vanishes with it, and nobody except her son seems to care or even notice. Although not as explicitly as in the play of perspectives explored above, the same strategy of textual separation is at work here. Not only do the many passersby remain oblivious to her tragedy, but, in the area surrounding the border-patrol station, Amelia's story is seen as no more than an everyday occurrence. At the same time, the moment is one of intense emotional investment on the part of the spectator. As is usual in Iñárritu's work, and is particularly intensified throughout the final part of *Babel*, the film brings us within inches of the characters, as if the barriers between the fictional world and ours could be dissolved. As Amelia and Luis embrace tightly, we may feel almost as if we are part of the loving gesture. Emotions become strongly physical as the characters come together in such a highly charged way, and we are invited to read into such moments a variety of feelings, from defeat and despondency at seeing one's past and present summarily erased to hope and faith in the power of love and the resilience of the human being and, more specifically, of the citizen of the borderland.

The dramatic weight of Amelia's plight flows uninterruptedly into the next narrative block. As Yussef looks at Ahmed's dead body being carried by the Moroccan police, the camera closes in on his face and circles around him to capture the misery of a child who has abruptly and tragically learned what love and loss are. This poignant close-up of Yussef prompts the only flashback in the film: a memory from the previous day in which the two Moroccan brothers, arms spread wide against the wind, share and revel in a moment of sheer joy (fig. 13). Yussef and Ahmed's game echoes an earlier scene in Chieko's storyline, in which the Japanese teenagers play out the "king of the world" scene in which Leonardo DiCaprio and Kate Winslet lean into the wind on the bow of the *Titanic* in James Cameron's 1997 film. While in the ultramodern big city the moment is a conscious reenactment of a well-known movie scene, the Moroccan boys, unaware of the filmic reference, surrender to the power of unmediated nature as they catch the wind with their arms outstretched. The scene does not only emphasize the physicality of this moment of communion between the characters but also brings

Figure 13. Happiness in flashback: Yussef and
Ahmed catch the wind in *Babel*.

to the fore how different the experience of early adolescence may be in
the two parts of the world.

The pleasant desert breeze gives way to the disruptive but much-
hoped-for wind caused by the helicopter landing in Tazarine. In a parallel
gesture to the one that got the rifle into Moroccan hands in the first
place, Richard tries to thank Anwar (Mohamed Akhzam) with a gift
of some dollar bills, which the latter rejects. Initially the U.S. citizen,
coming from a culture in which money has become a natural and conventional way to express affection and gratitude, especially towards those
less affluent, does not understand the guide's rejection, but, after his
wife's odyssey and near death, he only takes a few seconds to realize and
appreciate the wonder of less materialistic forms of human communication. Consistent with Iñárritu's views and with the conclusion of the rest
of the stories, physical contact in the form of another embrace becomes
a worthy substitute for bank bills. After this moment, we still see Richard at the hospital in Casablanca, in the sequence analyzed above, but
his parting from Anwar may be said to constitute his epiphany and the
culmination of his process of learning in the film, which immediately
links him to Amelia and Yussef and, shortly afterwards, to Chieko. Yet,
as in the case of the Moroccan and the Japanese teenagers, we cannot

help but notice the different repercussions of each of the characters' predicaments. Susan is evacuated from Tazarine under the attentive gaze of the villagers, who observe the whole process with curiosity and surprise. Even if their interest arises mainly from the novelty and extraordinariness of the technological display, the expectation generated by Susan's situation, which resonates all over the world, highly contrasts with the anonymity of Amelia's plight, which becomes a mere number in the immigration statistics. Our intense emotional engagement with each of these individual predicaments does not prevent the movie from signaling their different ramifications in order to articulate wider geopolitical concerns.

The emotional intensity of these final scenes is compounded by the extradiegetic music linking the three blocks and a similar use of shallow focus, which emphasizes vividly the human figures and their emotions, the blurring of the background rendering everything else irrelevant. As the musical score replaces dialogue in these three blocks, forging connections between people where verbal exchanges could not reach, the lack of a common language becomes less of a barrier to communication. Words, the film seems to argue, cannot come close to the power of deeply felt human contact in those moments of physical and emotional communion that constitute the film's drawn-out climax. At the end of *Babel,* a trauma caused by social and geopolitical circumstances brings characters into contact with their deep natures through an emotion that manifests itself physically and in an unmediated way. In the end, a globalized, deeply interconnected world simultaneously increases the chasms between people and has the power to make us realize what we still have in common.

These moments of heightened emotional investment in the plights of each of the characters are put into a wider perspective by the rest of the stories, which does not make characters' suffering less distressing but forces us to see them in the context of many other individual tragedies. This double drive is accurately captured in the final block and, more specifically, in its final scene. When Chieko's father, Yasujiro, comes back home from work, he finds his deaf-mute daughter naked on the balcony. Rebelliousness now turns into painful vulnerability as she grabs her father's hand, pleading for comprehension and affection. The estranged father and daughter finally reach out to each other through yet another embrace that, echoing and intensified by the climaxes of the previous stories, once again encapsulates the film's celebration of love and understanding against all odds (fig. 14). The girl's serious psychological problems are probably far from resolved, but at this moment of empathy with her father, they seem to have evaporated, along with, momentarily, the gap between generations.

It is at this point that the four narrative strands of the plot finally converge, the same physical gesture of affection and warmth summarizing the intimacy that links human beings across the continents. The film, however, does not end here. In accordance with the simultaneous drive to show each of the individual stories from a short and a long distance—both a microscopic and a macroscopic perspective—the camera pulls back from the two characters until, with the help of computer-generated imagery, they become invisible spots in the midst of the Tokyo night. Once again, through a combination of the two temporal paradigms discussed above, the film has brought us within inches of the characters to then drastically force us to look at them in a wider context, emphasizing how small and insignificant their stories seem when seen from a distance. Slowed down and emotionally charged chronological time has urged us to identify with the characters and their particular plights, whereas timeless time has put them into a broader perspective. Chieko

Figure 14. Redemption in the beautiful overpopulated city: Chieko and Yasujiro in *Babel*.

and her father's misery and isolation and the manifold feelings present in that final embrace lose momentum in the context of a beautiful and overpopulated city with hundreds of brightly lit windows that would probably reveal dramas similar to those narrated in this story. At the same time, the film's belief in the power of close human contact and the way the previous narrative blocks prepare the spectator for this final shot separate us from the individual incidents, conveying a more generalized feeling of hope in the potential of people for love in the midst of an indifferent, if not outright hostile, globalized society. The musical score chosen for this final scene, Ryuchi Sakamoto's "Bibo No Aozora"—which translates as "the beauty of the blue sky"—points in a similar direction. Reconciliation, redemption, and consolation may seem to be out of reach in an increasingly fractured world, but beauty and hope can still be found in our common humanity and in our ability to circumvent the obstacles that separate us. Sakamoto's melody seamlessly segues from Santaolalla's themes, particularly "Iguazu," which has linked the three previous blocks together. Its repetitive rhythms, which increase in intensity but never seem to reach a climax, aptly suggest that, as in other multiprotagonist films, the ending is just a stopping point, and tomorrow will bring new stories along.

Babel's sumptuous final shot, in its gradual separation from the high-rise balcony where Chieko and Yasujiro remain locked in one another's arms, appears to float over the nocturnal city, forever suspended in unbound space and time. As in the rest of the stories, chronological time advances slowly in this strand of the plot, seemingly unfolding every single detail of a day in the life of a traumatized teenager and bringing us ever closer to her tormented subjectivity. Slowing almost to a halt, linear chronology merges with the sense of immediacy intrinsic to timeless time, welding different temporalities in the overall structure of the film and locating them in an eternal present that defies the time sequence through the constant structural and thematic reverberations among the narrative blocks. Once the temporal sequence has been compressed through the film's particular approach to temporality, different chronological moments merge and fuse in an endless continuum, where feelings and emotions echo one another regardless of time and space. *Babel*'s ending leaves the spectator with a deep awareness of the importance of the multiple dramas of our contemporary world and of the huge rifts between places that, depending on the perspective, are as close to each other as they are separated, but also with a deep belief in our capacity to break barriers and come together through the universal language of the human heart.

Human Spaces in a Shrinking World

The construction of space is as central to the generic workings of multiprotagonist films as their use of temporal structures, but their formal deployment in Iñárritu's films calls the viewer's attention to two different and equally important dimensions of his art. If time is mainly, although not exclusively, articulated by means of complex narrative structures, space is most vividly conveyed through visual strategies. Although both levels of filmic construction and analysis are inevitably intertwined in the audiovisual narrative text, the Mexican director's complex approach to filmmaking recommends their separation in analysis. Narrative structure has constituted the focus of our analysis of filmic time in Iñárritu's movies; in the remaining two sections of this book we focus on stylistic elements and how they converge in the creation of space.

In Iñárritu's first three films, the idea of space varies from text to text as much as that of time. *Amores perros* separates the characters in three episodes and places them in three different spaces that intersect in the spot where the car accident takes place, and in various secondary places scattered throughout the narrative: the outside of the dog-fighting arena where el Chivo confronts Jarocho with his dogs at the beginning of the first episode, the street where the ex-terrorist passes Ramiro and Susana in the third episode, or the wall where the huge poster of Valeria is being taken down as el Chivo walks past. The film is about contemporary life in Mexico City, and the capital may be said to be its main subject. Conversely, the fictional city of *21 Grams* remains unnamed, but its forceful presence becomes a frame for, or even an expressionistic extension of, the characters' emotions and states of mind. In *Babel* the locations are again "real," as with the Mexico City of *Amores perros*, but they proliferate as the narrative moves between both sides of the San Diego–Tijuana border, two villages in Morocco, and Tokyo. The functions of the three filmic spaces are very different from one another, and so are the specific cinematic strategies that are used for their construction. In the following pages we would like to explore the ways in which space is constructed in Iñárritu's films and the cultural meanings it encompasses within the context of the multiprotagonist genre and contemporary cultural phenomena.

Space has often been defined in opposition to place, the opposition generally being between the abstract and the physical, or between the theoretical and the experienced. The geographer Yi-Fu Tuan, for example, explains that abstract space becomes concrete place as we familiarize ourselves with a town, a neighborhood, or a street (199). Space is an idea and place, an object; place is lived space. For Michel de Certeau, however, place is the order imposed by city planners, politicians, and those in power, and space is the way in which people experience that place by moving between different points and establishing intersections between different elements (117). It could be argued that film narratives construct space as part of their signifying structures, ascribing them various connotations and links with other elements such as events or characters. These abstract *spaces,* as Tuan would argue, are visualized and made concrete in specific *places*: the street of a city, the interior of a train, or the surface of an invented planet. Conversely, following de Certeau, these material places (in the sense that they can be perceived through the senses) remain lifeless and inert until they are turned into significant space by the network of meanings that the texts assign to them. Space, Manuel Castells argues, is the expression of society (440); therefore, the analysis of space casts light on the ways in which individuals relate to one another at a given historical juncture. Similarly, filmic space, although fictional, contains discourses and cultural attitudes toward human relationships. The Mexico City of *Amores perros* is not the same city analyzed by cultural critics, but the film does convey a certain view of life in the megalopolis at the beginning of the new century. The urban landscape of *21 Grams* is not a statement about a particular city so much as an abstract participant in the human relationships explored by the film. This cinematically constructed space becomes part of the web of meanings the text constructs around the ideas of death, solitude, and the urge to love others. In the shot analyzed at the beginning of this book, for example, space and character combine to suggest the feeling of unbearable loneliness experienced by Cristina.

For de Certeau, people turn places into spaces by experiencing them, by moving from one place to another, and by means of a myriad other urban practices (95). He conceives of the modern city as the ideal expression of lived space, but other configurations of space have become more relevant and more characteristic of contemporary society. Castells finds a novel conception of space as important as that of time to define the network society. He argues that people still live in places, whether cities or not, and perceive their space as place-based, but this "space of places" is being superseded by what he calls the "space of flows": a type of space in which geographical location and physical proximity are replaced by flows of information, work, capital and technology, across countries and continents (446). However, for Castells, not everybody has the same degree of access to the space of flows. The managerial elites are its main embodiment. They are cosmopolitan, whereas the rest of us are local, bound by our consciousness of belonging to a space of places (446). Yet groups and flows of people other than the industrial elites are also defined by the space of flows: migrations, diasporas, and tourism may not be so closely connected with communication networks, but they are as characteristic of the social structure of the modern world as those in charge of the information systems. The space of flows has reached every corner of our planet, and *Babel* is a powerful fictionalization of this phenomenon.

The space of flows defines the spatial configuration of many multi-protagonist movies. In *Babel,* characters are more or less firmly located in powerfully visualized places, and many of them are indeed defined by those places. But at the same time, they transcend their specific localities and are equally constructed through the narrative space of flows—the connections established between them across stories and geographical locations. In this film, as in other instances of the genre, space is a combination of places and flows. These flows take center stage, both when characters associated with different places interact in the course of the plot and when the film makes links proliferate between them through visual and narrative parallels and contrasts. As a consequence, a more intangible but very powerful space materializes that transcends the individual places and transforms them from autonomous and, in some cases, apparently remote locations into cogs of an intricate whole. With multiprotagonist structures that link characters living in the same city whose lives are brought together by a single event, *21 Grams* and

Amores perros use the space of flows just as centrally by encouraging spectators to infer their most important meanings from the growing number of connections between different strands of their plots. The cities in these films are therefore both geographical places where the characters live and chains of flows that are superimposed on their streets and buildings.

Mean Streets

Amores perros does not offer a stereotyped view of Mexico or its capital. The director has often explained that he was attempting to counteract folkloric representations of his country and show life as it is: "Not the Taco Bell idea" (qtd. in Hirschberg 34). Consequently, the Mexico City that we see here is, according to many critics, one never seen before on film (Smith, *Amores* 50). While some reviewers still complained about the nagging presence of received ideas about Mexican society (Rich 34) and about the limited reach of its social canvas, others celebrated its ambition to cover all social strata (Romney, "Buy One"). The multiprotagonist format, with its proliferation of stories in a single narrative, often encourages such impressions of inclusiveness. When the genre is used, as it often happens in contemporary cinema, to tell several stories that take place in one city, a frequent tendency is to understand the different plots as having been carefully chosen to convey a sense of the whole of the city in its manifold dimensions and intricacies.

In the case of *Amores perros,* it may seem too bold to affirm that three episodes, no matter how ambitious their reach, may accurately represent the totality of the urban experience of a megalopolis of more than twenty million people. Given the complexities of the ever-growing and ever-fluctuating population of Mexico City, three social strata (assuming that each story represents a clearly differentiated social group) do not begin to cover a fraction of its totality. The film is also an avowedly urban film that articulates the human and communal conflicts that characterize contemporary cities, including poverty, corruption, and violence, while at the same time portraying experiences that would be difficult to export to other urban spaces. In this sense, its focus is very much the Mexican capital, both in what it shares with and what differentiates it from other big cities. The movie inscribes itself within the recent trend of an unprecedented awareness of the city in Mexican cinema (Foster

159). Yet, given its critical reception and its reputation as portraying a different type of Mexico for contemporary audiences, the way in which it constructs its space may seem paradoxical. As Paul Julian Smith elaborates, none of the architectural distinctiveness of the capital, like its combination of ancient and modern buildings, and certainly none of its tourist attractions are ever visible in the film. In fact, with the exception of a distant view, shaky and blurred, of the Latin American Tower during the car chase, there is not one recognizable building in sight (*Amores* 51–52). For Jeff Menne, the society delineated by the film is partitioned into private spaces (76). Its vivid picture of urban life is mostly conveyed through the relationship between the characters and their immediate surroundings. In this case, rather than space offering a geographical, social, or psychological frame for human interactions, it is those human interactions that make up the space. With the usual abundance of close-ups and extreme close-ups in Iñárritu's films, Mexico City is to some extent written on the characters' faces and bodies.

At the same time, that representation is not neutral and is not carried solely by the actors' performances. Among the formal elements employed by *Amores perros* to both unify the different spaces and convey their specificities and their individual contribution to the development of the plot is the constant use of a short focal length or wide angle. The proliferation of the wide angle, along with its opposite, the longer lenses that flatten the image, is, according to David Bordwell, one of the characteristics of intensified continuity, the new style of filmmaking that he sees as a modern development of classical continuity. Looming close-ups, expansive establishing shots, cramped interiors, and foreground-background interplay are among the functions of the shorter focal length (*The Way* 125). In his book on Stanley Kubrick, a director well known for his consistent use of this stylistic option, James Naremore describes its effect as creating "an eerie, distorted, sometimes caricatured sense of space" (25). Iñárritu's intention in this film is never to caricature but to present space and characters from a hyperrealistic perspective, one related to the pervasive presence of violence and its manifold consequences as a defining characteristic of contemporary life in his native city. In interviews Iñárritu has insisted that Mexico City is a violent place, emotionally and physically, a city that has lost its sense of humanity and is about to be taken over by our animal nature (Niogret 26). The selective use of short focal lengths is one of the visual devices he employs to convey this perspective. In the hands of the Mexican filmmaker and his director of photography, Rodrigo Prieto, the wide angle is not just a marker of a contemporary director. Like other elements of visual style employed by the film, it becomes a rhetorical figure with diverse and complex functions, reflecting the two levels of meaning making in multiprotagonist narratives. Visual strategies repeated from one episode to the next intensify the links that spectators are able to make between them, guaranteeing our understanding of the text as a game of multiple reflections in which meaning is never exhausted by one single event, character, or narrative. These visual styles are never identical, are often contextualized differently, and consequently acquire specific meanings. This diversity multiplies the reach of the multiprotagonist text beyond any single, unifying interpretation and, in the case of *Amores perros,* suggests that the city produces an infinite number of meanings, all of them interrelated but all of them different.

The wide angle is used in *Amores perros* in conjunction with other devices that distort the filmic space or, rather, create a space characterized by a dehumanizing violence. Handheld camera, low and high angles, and canted shots all combine with the wide angle to convey a sense of, in the words of Françoise Audée, "explosive incandescence" (22). For different reasons, life in the tiny, humble house where Octavio and Susana live, in the much more up-market and sunny apartment that Daniel has just bought to start his new life with Valeria, and in the dilapidated basement that el Chivo shares with his dogs is under constant threat of detonation, and the frequent resort to the wide-angle lens ensures that we never abandon that impression. Yet the individual reasons for the persistence of this feeling are as important as the overall impression, and the wide angle proves a powerful unifying device and one that is capable of signifying differently depending on the narrative context. The analysis of several shots and sequences from various moments in the film will illustrate this textual approach.

Family relationships in the first episode are defined by the cramped space of the house shared by four adults and a baby. Octavio's intense desire for his sister-in-law, Susana's ambivalent attitude toward him, Ramiro's violent machismo, and their mother's growing hostility toward Susana and fraught love for Ramiro could all be seen as a consequence of the way their scarce economic means have thrown them together in the suffocating confinement of their domestic space. An early scene shows the two brothers arriving and joining the other three in the kitchen. This sequence is visually articulated by means of close-ups of the characters, often accompanied, as usual in Iñárritu, by out-of-focus shapes of other characters in the foreground and background and punctuated by establishing shots of the whole group. These shots are composed in three planes, emphasizing the distances and relationships between the characters: Susana holding the baby in the foreground, Octavio in the middle ground, and Concha and Ramiro moving in and out of the frame in the back (fig. 15). This perspective prioritizes the bourgeoning of illicit but inevitable desire between the first two, the hovering presence of a husband and brother who is too aggressively narcissistic to notice what is going on, and a mother who suspects even before anything happens. The short focal length distorts foreground and background; increases the distance between Octavio and Susana, on the one hand, and Ramiro and Concha, on the other hand; and emphasizes the proliferation of objects between the characters, like so many obstacles to healthy communication between them. Although the wide angle may appear to exaggerate the size of the room, the impression of distorted family life predominates,

Figure 15. The distorted family romance
of *Amores perros*.

excessive proximity increasing the confusion between different types of relationships and shaping the specific contours of the potential urban explosiveness in this part of town.

In this scene, a short focal length is used in the establishing shots, but the close-ups are generally spared. Later in the episode, it appears also in the shorter distances, making our sense of space even more suffocating. When, toward the end of the episode, Concha tells Octavio first that Ramiro was beaten up the previous night and then that he has left the house with Susana and the baby, the tension between mother and son, their cruelty and psychological aggressiveness toward one another, and their despair are compounded by the distortion of their facial features produced by the wide angle. In contrast with this exchange of fraught close-ups, the scene ends with a long shot of Octavio standing by the window of Susana's bedroom, in which the wide angle, accompanied by a high angle and slightly shaking handheld camera, conveys both the character's extreme frustration and the violence that is about to blow up (fig. 16). Suddenly, the house has become empty and unbearably huge, in spite of its tiny size, as Octavio's plans have been unexpectedly and, from his perspective, inexplicably thwarted. The wide angle has served to contract and expand the space, depending on the family dynamics,

Figure 16. Unbearable loneliness in wide angle: Octavio in *Amores perros.*

both operations unified by the sense of a social and economic space that keeps human beings on edge and brings out violence, cruelty, and destructive impulses.

This sense of explosive incandescence reaches its climax in the scene in which Octavio stabs his dog-fighting rival Jarocho to death, after the latter has shot Cofi in the middle of a fight with his own dog. We are now outside the family house, but the two spaces are unified by the wide angle. At the same time, the visual articulation contrasts with the former scene. In a film with a low average shot length (4.9 seconds), long takes are scarce. The most spectacular one happens now, as Octavio carries his wounded dog out of the pit, puts it in his car, goes back in and stabs his rival, and then runs back to the car, followed by Jarocho's men, and drives off. The chase that ensues will culminate in the crash into Valeria's car. This long take lasts approximately sixty seconds, and again the wide angle is part of a visual strategy that includes high angle and nervously handheld camera, the shakiness of the camera increasing as the character walks back into the arena and then runs out. The shot is offered both as a pointed contrast with the previously described one and as a consequence of it. Octavio's bottled-up feelings after Susana's disappearance are transformed into horror at seeing Cofi badly wounded. The nervous stasis of the earlier shot explodes in a flurry of apparently senseless movement: out of the building, in again, out again. The use of the short focal length suggests that Octavio's feeling of loss continues unabated, his momentary inability to react in the previous scene now replaced by an irrational action that can only lead to further aggravation.

Again, the use of this stylistic option in both scenes guarantees visual consistency as a way to articulate character psychology, but in its association with a static image first and an extremely kinetic one later, it conveys different stages in the downward spiral that constitutes the character's narrative journey. Additionally, the wide angle is as closely linked with the interior space and constraints on liberty of movement in the first case as it is with fast and decisive action in the second one, a contrast that underlines the connections between social and psychological curtailment of freedom. In general, this rhetorical figure constructs a space for the first episode that cramps the characters in tiny interiors, constantly impairs their personal or social progress, and surrounds them with an air of inevitability and foreboding from which they are unable to escape.

At the beginning of the second episode, featuring Daniel and Valeria, wide-angle frames seem to have disappeared; they only start creeping in again when the couple returns home, she in the wheelchair, after the accident. From this moment onward, shorter focal lengths gradually change our perception of the new apartment, which at first sight contrasts vividly, in its openness and airiness, with Octavio and Susana's house. While the latter is consistently seen as a constraining space, the expensive apartment of the second episode changes shape as the narrative develops. A wide-angle high-angle shot of Valeria lying impotent on her bed as she hears that her contract has been canceled because of her broken leg is an early indication of things to come, as the comfortable apartment suddenly acquires the appearance of a suffocating cage. The final sequence of the episode is a good illustration of this visual versatility. After having had her leg amputated, Valeria comes back home for the second time and heads directly for the living-room window. Earlier in the film, we had seen both her and Daniel looking out of this window at the huge poster of her advertising campaign, a symbol of a past identity that now seems forever lost. The distance between the entrance door and the window as she moves from one to the other is visually exaggerated by means of a combination of changes in focal length between shots, editing (the various cuts make her progress seem longer), and mise-en-scène (the original hole in the wooden floor has now expanded as various other boards have also disappeared after Daniel's final attempt at rescuing her dog, Richi). At the end of this metaphorical journey, Valeria breaks into tears when she sees the space formerly occupied by her image now empty except for a telephone number awaiting the next poster of the next model. The model's identity was literally all image, all surface, and now that the image has disappeared there seems to be nothing left but a blank. In fact, as she wheels her chair toward the window, the apartment acquires the appearance of a tunnel, at the end of which there is no exit (fig. 17).

Yet, all is not lost. After the couple's bitter argument that led to her losing her leg, and Daniel's temptation to go back to his wife, they are still together, the two perhaps beginning to search for alternative values on which to build a renewed relationship. Santaolalla's sound track, as well as lighting, costume, and actor performance, begin to suggest that the future may not be all pessimistic. Once Valeria reaches the window, the

Figure 17. Threatening space: Valeria
and Daniel in *Amores perros.*

film frames her from behind in long shot, while Daniel comes onscreen and joins her by the window, metaphorically locking his life to hers and hinting that a new, stronger, more authentic identity may be found for the two of them in a more profound love, based on the deeper values acquired during their passage through the tunnel. The leisurely musical theme that now resumes reinforces the feeling of a new romantic and spiritual balance in the making for the couple, a deeper level of communication than they had been able to achieve before. Shortly after, the film returns to a similar long shot, but now some changes are apparent. The frame distance has increased slightly, the characters being now a little further from the spectator; the handheld camera begins to shake perceptibly; a subtly disturbing sound as of something being dragged on the floor can be heard under the continuing string music; and, most obviously, the focal length has been shortened considerably, turning the room that only a few seconds before seemed to welcome their reconciliation into a visibly distorted, threatening space again. Finally, to close the shot and the episode, a second before the shot fades to black, a telephone is heard ringing. This turns out to be the ring of Gustavo's cell phone, a sound bridge to the beginning of the third episode, but for a moment, the spectator may infer that it is the last of a series of anonymous telephone calls that pepper this story and have become a motif representing the volatility of heterosexual relationships. Thus, this final sound effect provides an interpretation of the change in focal length, suggesting again the couple's precariousness and, therefore, the extreme fragility of Valeria's blossoming new identity. The wide angle in this final shot is consistent with the previous visual treatment of the apartment, but at the same time, the text uses the spectator's unconscious familiarity with it to convey subtle narrative changes and to provide a combination of faint hope and continuing uneasiness for the dénouement of this strand of the plot.

When his cell phone rings at the beginning of the final story, Gustavo is on his way to hire el Chivo to assassinate his half-brother and business partner, accompanied by Leonardo (José Sefami), a corrupt policeman who once sent the ex-revolutionary to jail and is now his friend and associate. The scene that follows, in which arrangements are made for the murder, takes place inside el Chivo's "living room" and is fully shot in wide angle, both the establishing shot and the otherwise classical analytical breakdown formed by alternating medium shots and close-ups of the three characters. The establishing shot, which is repeated at the end of the sequence, frames the characters frontally and from a slightly high angle. The short lens not only distorts space in a general sense but also arranges the characters along divergent lines that exaggerate the distance between them and make their conversation seem fantastic, almost grotesque. Any hope of communication and community in a society thus conceptualized is rapidly slipping away along visual lines that, with a normal focal length, would have been parallel. When the text moves to single shots of the three participants in this warped exchange, the wide angle forces us to reflect on the social reality they represent: el Chivo's manic laughter underscores the potential violence ready to explode at every turn; Gustavo's affluent, good-boy looks contrast with the moral viciousness engendered by money and ambition; and Leonardo's monstrously distorted face becomes a compendium of the urban hell that his corruption stands for. If *Amores perros* makes an attempt at social inclusiveness, this is perhaps the most obvious moment, and the result is a picture of a city seriously ill and with scant prospects of release.

The proliferation of extreme focal lengths is, as Bordwell points out, a signifier of contemporary cinema, but in the hands of Iñárritu and Prieto, the wide angle becomes a powerful tool in the construction of an urban space that is strongly unified in the intense feeling of violence and pervasive danger that it conveys and in the suggestion of the social conditions that produce such violence. At the same time, the wide-angle space is diversified to express the variety of scenarios of the modern megalopolis and to narrate the multiple stories that constitute it within its multiprotagonist canvas. The visual consistency and the versatility of the formal device make it suitable to portray the ebullient, ever-changing, multishaped urban monster. Several exterior shots at the end of the film—including the one of el Chivo driving past the huge wall from which the poster of Valeria is being taken down (fig. 5) and others that show him driving Gustavo's car to the garage where he sells it and walking out of the city accompanied only by Cofi—are conspicuously shot in wide angle, contradicting the general norm that the film had set itself for this episode. It is as if, although he has abandoned his dwellings permanently, el Chivo continues to carry with him the monstrous space, spreading it wherever he passes and confirming the narrative status of his character and his house as distorted symbols of the whole city. At the same time, the deep, if denaturalized, open space constructed by the short lens appears to carry now a faint glimmer of hope, the low-angle view of the character decisively walking away into the horizon before the film definitively fades to black conjuring up traditional connotations of new lives lying ahead. Once again, the versatile visual strategy has changed its meaning in order to represent yet one more facet of the chameleonic city.

City of Light

21 Grams was filmed on location in Memphis, Tennessee, and in the outskirts of Albuquerque, New Mexico. In its fictional world, however, the setting of the action is never mentioned, and the two shooting locations are collapsed into a single, unidentified town. The filmmakers have repeatedly insisted on the relevance of this anonymous space. After abandoning his initial idea of filming the story in Mexico City, Iñárritu was not interested in exploring life in any particular place across the border but, rather, was striving for something more abstract. Memphis (and New Mexico) gave him a certain personality, certain textures (Calhoun) that spectators would be familiar with from other filmic representations. The film intersperses long shots of streets and buildings, including recognizable Memphis sites like the Hernando de Soto Bridge and the Arcade Diner, but in general, even more than *Amores perros*, it focuses on the bodies and especially the faces of the characters, with a handheld camera that accompanies them everywhere in close distance, scrutinizes them, and wobbles and shakes with them in an attempt to capture even the minutest expression of their emotions.

It is mostly, although not exclusively, in the gaps between the characters, in the geography of their faces, and in the links established between them by the narrative structure and the editing patterns analyzed above that the filmic space materializes. Therefore, this space is largely drawn on the actors' bodies and performances; but, as in the previous movie, other strategies are also summoned to create a powerful sense of a space that exists halfway between the physical and the emotional. Extreme focal lengths, for example, continue to be used here, but the distinctive look of the film is more visibly constructed around the contrasts between different stocks and colors for the three main characters; the use of very bright, sometimes blinding lighting; and the bleach-bypass or silver-retention process. This technique consists in retaining the silver in the processing of a color film, although the result can also be achieved digitally. The final effect gives the impression of a black-and-white image superimposed onto a color image and intensifies contrast and graininess. The process, which had already been used in *Amores perros* and would be used again, although differently, in *Babel*, gives the film a desaturated, contrastive feeling. The combination of these strategies suggests a recognizable yet otherworldly fictional universe that harbors a variety of intense, primary emotions and desires. The bleach bypass, the anonymity of the unnamed city, the tight framings, and the insistent handheld camera, as well as the "denaturalized" sense of time, divest *21 Grams* of much contextual detail and demand a novel approach to the understanding of filmic space.

The stripping-down of background elements together with the proliferation of stories, characters, and temporal points of reference recalls some of the tenets of actor network theory. According to Bruno Latour, society is not a given, a background, or a context but something that is constantly created, re-created, and transformed through associations between actors. Society does not preexist individual, temporally bound connections between actors. Rather, it is the actors that make up the social

(36). This also evokes the space theorized by de Certeau, his ghost cities becoming lived through the people that inhabit them, their movements, and other practices, in another theory that downplays context (which he calls "place") and focuses on everyday experience. The emphasis placed by these two authors on relationships, links, and flows between people as the basis of all social organization, as well as the provisionality, instability, and fluidity of the network thus created, echoes descriptions of the multiprotagonist genre and perhaps helps explain its current popularity. It is in this sense, as well as through its complex temporal structure, that a film like *21 Grams* relates to the genre most deeply. The creation of a space almost exclusively around emotional links between the characters, whether they are physically together in the frame or in different places, articulates a particular type of society that in a fictional universe dominated by intense feelings seems to be uninterested in whatever falls outside the characters' predicaments and more or less desperate attempts at making significant contact with one another.

In *21 Grams,* intense white light and silver retention most conspicuously distance the filmic space from photographic realism. The film starts and finishes with the moments previous to Paul's death of heart failure. At the beginning, he is barely surviving, as his heart rapidly deteriorates, whereas the transplant gives him a brief new lease on life, during which his fleeting but powerful relationship with Cristina develops. It could therefore be argued that for this brief period he has come back from the dead, to where he will soon return. The sudden and shocking loss of her daughters and husband brings Cristina also into close contact with death. While the film's final images may suggest that she is beginning to come out of the tunnel, the only respite that she is given in the rest of the movie from her extreme and uncomprehending bereavement is that provided by her desire for Paul. However, this desire, like Paul's for her, is strongly mediated by Michael's heart and could be said to have a necrophiliac dimension. Jack's fundamentalism keeps him constantly in touch with his own mortality as well, and his role in the narrative revolves around his accidental killing of three people, his near death at Paul's hands, and his involvement in Paul's death. Death is never far away, and the provisionality of the characters' identities is closely linked to their awareness of mortality and of the ephemerality of life. The defamiliarizing function of bright lighting and silver retention is related to this perspective: suffering and bereavement are acute in the constant presence of death, but this very experience makes the characters' desires stronger, their search for affection more relentless, their wish to reach out to other human beings more unstoppable. The protagonists of 21 Grams find the strength to carry on living in the certainty that death is always, sometimes literally, around the corner. The proliferation of comparable experiences revolving around the car accident, combined with the drastic minimalism of the filmic space, enlarge the canvas of human relationships and zero in on what is common to all of them, while the focus on connections, parallels, transfers, and mediations speaks to the contemporary relevance of the multiprotagonist genre.

In Iñárritu's second film, space and time are closely connected in terms of narrative construction. In their brief moment of happiness during their date at the restaurant, Paul explains to Cristina the power of numbers, and she smiles contentedly at the poetic quality of his vision (fig. 18). This glimpse of ephemeral bliss is underscored by lighting. Around them not only the empty restaurant but also most colors have become redundant, and only the man, the woman, and the intense bright light around them remain. As the frame pulls closer and closer to the characters in the shot/reverse shot sequence, the light coming through the window surrounds them with an aura of purity and well-being. A cut then takes us outside and shows the couple walking to her house later in the afternoon, the dazzling light of the sun coming through the wintry trees, reinforcing the presence of a magic space between the prospective lovers. The lighting pattern of this scene may remind viewers of the film's opening shot and lead us to place that moment chronologically shortly after this scene, as a logical consequence of their obvious mutual affection and attraction (fig. 19). Yet what we get instead when the walk concludes is a sequence narrating a later moment, when they are together in the motel room and Paul is ready to go out and kill Jack (fig. 11).

The motel shot is so similar to the film's initial shot that the spectator may at first think that it is indeed the same shot, now repeated in chronological sequence. We see the two characters in similar positions to the previous one, and framing and perspective are approximately the same. But the differences soon become as obvious as the similarities. For one thing, the space around them has completely changed: the serenity conferred by the dazzling white light in the earlier shot is replaced by

Figures 18–19. The light of ephemeral happiness:
Cristina and Paul in *21 Grams.*

gloom and anguish, conveyed through a combination of the half-light coming through the partly drawn curtains and the bleach bypass that has now reappeared, intensifying the contrast, defamiliarizing the mise-en-scène, and, specifically here, emphasizing the light that falls on Paul's face. This may be, like the one at the beginning of the film, a postcoital scene, but with very different connotations: the relationship between the two characters that was a minute before characterized by affection and desire has suddenly gravitated toward anxiety and death again. Cristina's revenge wish has changed the nature of her relationship with Paul, who is now about to embark on his frustrated attempt to kill Jack. We are not aware of any of this yet, nor do we know why the expressions on the characters' faces have changed so drastically from one shot to the next. Iñárritu and Arriaga's fractured structure practically superimposes the two spaces, fusing them as two sides of the same emotional universe, love and death becoming intensely intertwined.

In this case, visual reverberations not only link different shots within the film but also transcend the text, evoking one of its most obvious intertexts, Nan Goldin's photo series *The Ballad of Sexual Dependency* and, more specifically, one of its most celebrated items, "Nan and Brian in Bed." Iñárritu and his collaborators have often referred to the influence of Goldin's art on his films (Wood 78), but in *21 Grams* the visual quotation is explicit. With a woman (the photographer herself) lying on a bed and a man sitting up and smoking a cigarette, presumably after having had sex, both in similar positions to Cristina and Paul in the two shots from the film, the photo suggests a relationship in deep crisis. Sex appears not to have brought about understanding and happiness but tension, anxiety, rejection, and suffering. In Goldin's series, sex is sometimes a joyful experience, but at this point the emphasis is on the impossibility of communication between two human beings and the fragility that sexual tension produces in one of the partners. The publication of the series in book form places this photograph in its final section of seven shots, inaugurating a sequence that includes, for example, a shot of ruffled, empty beds, and one of two skeletons coupling, as well as a frame of two graves in Mexico (Goldin 137–43). The second item in this section is particularly apposite for our analysis in its even closer resemblance to Iñárritu's two framings. The shot, entitled "Couple in Bed," shows again a man and a woman, but the perspective is closer to the film's two shots with the woman naked in the foreground (awake in this case), and her face turned away from the man, who is half-dressed and sits on the corner of the bed in a pensive pose. The rift between the lovers here is even more pronounced, and it is ironically compounded by the photo of the empty beds that follows this one. In this sequence, the link between sex and death is pervasive, in dramatic and comic forms.

Iñárritu's visual quotation, however, is not simply a tribute to the New York photographer he admires; it is a powerful way of constructing a different type of interpersonal relationship on the basis of the connotations of the original text. In *21 Grams* the connections between love and death are also ever-present, but they are more ambivalent. The film edits together the beginning of the relationship and the couple's stay at the motel via our memory of the first shot and constructs a continuous space that transcends geography to bring home its view of existence: distressing experiences and acute suffering bring us together, but human resilience and the will to reach out to the other allow us to find happiness and peace in desire, affection, and other forms of interpersonal communication. Yet, as the film's fractured narrative structure also underlines, such intense links never last long, since they contain in themselves the germ of decay and the shadow of death. Love and pain are inextricably intertwined; hope and despair inevitably follow one another.

This close connection between despair and hope is suggested in the motel shot through the combination of silver retention and harsh lighting on Paul's face. The presence of Sean Penn's character throughout the movie is articulated through various shades of this combination, a spectrum that links his familiarity with death with the glimmer of hope that his narrative development casts on himself and other characters. Whereas in the scene just analyzed the proximity of death is brought to the fore, especially given the expression on his face and the reason that has taken the couple to the motel, in other cases the balance may lean in a different direction. For example, when Paul finally confesses to Cristina that he is carrying Michael's heart, she is overwhelmed by the news and throws him out of her house. He stays in the street inside his car all night, and when she wakes up the next morning and sees that he is still there she joins him and they finally make up.

The sequence of shots inside the car can be seen as a distillation of the way in which space is articulated in *21 Grams:* a series of close-ups and extreme close-ups of the characters' faces, scrutinizing every detail and changing emotion, lit with artificially enhanced natural lighting, and manipulated in postproduction through bleach bypass, which brings an extra edge to the wintry atmosphere (fig. 20). At the same time, these formal devices lift the scene from reality into a parallel realm of heightened feelings in which life-giving forces coexist with the death drive but, on this occasion, win the battle, as is represented by their final kiss halfway between reconciliation and sexual desire. The use of

Figure 20. A love sprung from the certainty
of mortality: Cristina in *21 Grams*.

cinematography is not very distant here from the establishing shot of
the motel, yet the connotations are drastically different. Filmic space
has shrunk to the distance between the two front seats of a car and between two people struggling with their deepest fears while discovering
the powerful currents that have started to flow between them. Put at
the service of this construction of space, harsh light and silver retention erase realistic details and turn the situation into an abstraction of
a love that has sprung from the certainty of mortality. The narrative
context remains crucial to understand how they got here, but the film's
statement transcends the individual characters and their stories, the
sequence becoming a powerful visualization of the line of the poem
Paul had mentioned to Cristina at the restaurant. The sequence then
segues almost immediately into the bedroom, where the two lovers are
shown finally consummating their desire, the bright white light once
again taking over to convey both the extent of the sexual passion and the
abstract and universal quality of this particular encounter. Throughout
the film, Iñárritu and Prieto subtly modify this blend of bleach bypass
and lighting strategies to suggest a palette of feelings and psychological
states. At the same time, they keep at its emotional core the human urge
to love and affect other people's lives while remaining, as we always are,
in the clutches of suffering and death.

Iñárritu's ambitious perspective is not only put forward abstractly through such formal devices but also through the inextricability of space and time within the framework of the multiprotagonist genre. Thus common experiences are expanded through the proliferation of links between characters and situations. Cristina and Paul's transition from the car to the bedroom is not made directly but via two brief shots of Mary arriving home and then sitting despondently in her and Paul's apartment. The shallow focus of the first shot, although in long distance, reminds us of the same technique used in the shots/reverse shots of Paul and Cristina inside the car, whereas the short-focal-length high angle of the second one underscores the character's unbearable loneliness, the light falling on her face enhanced by the bleach bypass, ironically linking Mary's feelings with her husband's in the motel shot previously discussed. The point of this transition is precisely the establishment of links between characters and spaces. Mary's space is related to Paul and Cristina's both narratively and visually, and the spectator is compelled to explore the more obvious reverberations and side-effects of the newly formed couple's love affair and the treelike structure of human relationships with new, interrelated life experiences constantly branching off in expected and unexpected directions.

The tenuous barrier between love and death is also apparent in the scenes involving Jack, which often link him to Paul and Cristina. After the shot inside the room at the motel, Paul goes out, accosts Jack, forces him to walk away from the motel, and fires his gun at him. The final two shots of the scene are a close-up of the gun firing in the direction of the spot where Jack is kneeling on the ground and of Paul's face as he pulls the trigger three times. Instead of the expected reverse shot of Jack being wounded by the bullets, the film cuts to a tight framing of a woman's crotch as a man's hand goes up her skirt. We soon realize that the man and woman are Jack and Marianne having sex after he has returned from jail. Given the screen direction suggested by the cut, it feels almost as if Paul has shot the woman's genitals, Jack's hand materializing as an extension of the gun. Rather than prompting a traditional feminist reading of heterosex being represented in patriarchal discourses as an act of extreme male violence on women—an interpretation that seems conspicuously out of place here—the false reverse shot links as closely and as strikingly as the film can manage Jack's near-death experience (later we find out that Paul has not shot him) and sexual passion.

This link is compounded narratively because the intensity of the encounter is also presented as a release of the tension caused by the car accident, as a consequence of which three people have been killed. Unlike earlier examples, the space appears to be continuous from one scene to the next, lighting and bleach bypass, as well as nervous handheld camera and furious cutting, ensuring a certain degree of visual homogeneity between two scenes that are temporally and spatially distant. Jack and Marianne's harrowing relationship is marked by his deep existential doubts and his struggle to come to terms with his place in the world in the face of all the suffering and death surrounding him. Love and death exist for him in the same emotional space, and the text appears to be suggesting that moments of heightened awareness of his mortality energize his sexual desire. At the same time, the construction of homogeneous as well as diverse spaces around the different characters' desires allows spectators to relate comparable experiences and speculate on the range of possibilities.

In general, as the film moves between different places and times, linking them together in a single emotional space, formal strategies direct spectators to explore the intricacies of this space and the ways in which connections trigger new developments. Single experiences, causes, and consequences are constantly rejected by multiprotagonist movies, which attempt to capture the complexity of experience by calling attention to webs of meanings and to the increasingly composite nature of human identity. Iñárritu uses multiprotagonist structures and a rich panoply of formal strategies to redirect our interest from the individual places and characters to the links between them: from the space of places to the space of flows. In *Babel,* both spaces are to some extent collapsed into one, since part of its action happens in the borderland, a place whose existence makes sense only, at least initially, as a space of flows; a space that, through the filmmaker's deployment of the conventions of the multiprotagonist genre, becomes a powerful signifier of contemporary identity.

Al otro lado

In *Amores perros,* Octavio never manages to realize his plan to move to Ciudad Juárez with Susana and her baby. We last see him at the bus station in Mexico City, hopelessly waiting for her before boarding the bus that would have taken them north to a life together. A heart-breaking long take (not dissimilar formally from the one in *21Grams* described at the beginning of this book) racks focus from a close-up of the character's face, still bearing the wounds from the car accident, to the bus driver in the background, and back to him. Still in the same shot he turns around, spent and defeated, and hobbles back, disappearing into the anonymous throng of the city night as Santaolalla's elegiac notes are mysteriously joined by a faintly heard Mariachi-like melody to compound the diverse strands of the character's heartbreak. Octavio is not yet ready to leave the city and travel north, and, metaphorically, neither is the film. The lyrics of the rap song "Amores perros: De perros amores" by Control Machete, which is not part of the text but was used for the trailer and the DVD menus, include, at the beginning, the following line: "Olvidamos que para llegar al otro lado hay que empezar derribando el primero de los muros" (We forget that to get to the other side we must start by demolishing the first of the walls). In Mexico, the phrase "el otro lado" has very specific connotations, usually meaning the other side of the northern border. It is tempting therefore to interpret this line biographically and argue that, like Octavio, Iñárritu was not ready yet to cross to the other side and, for his first feature film, in spite of the looming presence of the notorious border town as an uncertain project of Octavio's, he decided to remain within the confines of his home city. In retrospect, this proved a wise decision; *Amores perros* became a powerful representation of the director's home town at the dawn of the new century and derived its transnational appeal from its specific geographical localization.

The confinement did not last long. Iñárritu and Arriaga took their second Mexican story to the other side of the border and turned it into a U.S. film. Iñárritu himself followed in the steps of millions of Mexicans before him and moved to Los Angeles with his family. Earlier border crossers themselves, neither Alfonso Cuarón nor Guillermo del Toro had dealt directly with the issue of immigration in any of their films, and, from the evidence of his first two movies, Iñárritu appeared to follow the same path. *Babel* changed this: not only does one of the four strands of its plot take place wholly within the space of the border between Mexico and the United States, but the border crossings directly featured in this segment affect the rest of the characters in the other spaces and construct a world traversed by material and metaphorical borders. *Babel* is a multilayered border film that urges spectators to reflect on the numerous and complex dimensions of the concept and the reality of the border. As in the other two films, the director employs a series of formal strategies to construct this particular space. We would like to explore all of these dimensions and follow Iñárritu's trajectory from the capital city to the northern border, and from there to the representation of various facets of the transnational in today's global society.

In our earlier discussion of the concept of *mexicanidad* and its significance in Iñárritu's *oeuvre*, there was a missing ingredient: the border—*la frontera*—and its presence in Mexican history, in the definition of national identity, and in the Mexican collective psyche. As Carlos González Gutiérrez has argued, the Mexican nation extends beyond the territory contained by its borders, comprising a diaspora of which, uniquely among the nations of the world, 98.5 percent resides in the United States (545). The two-thousand-mile line between the two countries separates those living on either side of it but also creates a continuum between them and a complex sense of identity that, consciously in many cases but unconsciously in many others, affects the way in which they think about themselves and, literally, about their place in the world. "El otro lado" is ever present in contemporary Mexican culture, and, although the vast majority of people of Mexican origin living in the United States do not think of themselves as descendants of the original Mexicans who suddenly became part of another country in the mid-nineteenth century, their cultural distinctiveness sets them aside from other communities north of the border.

Mexico is a nation historically and culturally defined by its northern border, and the massive presence of people of Mexican origin on both of its sides expands that border into a particularly vibrant and complex borderland. As anybody traveling from one country to the other will immediately notice, the differences between both sides are enormous. Yet the great variety of individual circumstances, the multiple crossings and types of crossings taking place every day, and the extremely fluid shape of the influx of Mexican citizens into the United States make it impossible to impose a drastic separation between north and south, pointing instead to the growing number and depth of individual and cultural exchanges, as well as conflicts, throughout the region.

This distinctive culture has also produced a history of cinematic representations. Classical U.S. cinema often constructed the southern border as the threshold to a fantasy world of escape from the frustrations and repressions of civilized and/or corrupt society. The Western is the genre that dramatizes these fantasies most powerfully and most frequently. According to Camilla Fojas, the Western genre uses the southern frontier, as it had used the western frontier, to delineate and define "America" and to reaffirm "core American values" (2 and 27). Mexican cinema has traditionally sought to both downplay the weight of the northern neighbor's influence in its constructions of national identity and turn border crossings into habitual and uneventful facts of everyday life for Mexicans and U.S. Americans.

One of the most loved comics of Mexican cinema, Tin-Tan, was nicknamed "el pachuco del cine mexicano." He embodied in his films the cross-border component of *mexicanidad*. In one of his most popular films, *El hijo desobediente* (The Disobedient boy; 1945), he travels from the northern state of Chihuahua to Mexico City, dressed in a zoot suit, to become a famous singer. His eventual success is closely linked to his hybrid identity, which is seen, for once, as a viable version of *mexicanidad*, embodied principally in his use of language ("los States," "Sorry," jefe," "no estoy joking," "bueno, so long," "que me des un kiss") and in his singing (he asserts, for example, that "Allá en el Rancho Grande," one of the best-loved Mexican songs, is a "canción chicana"). This movie both celebrates hybridity and papers over deep-held anxieties that in the course of history have often come to the surface more aggressively. This was, for example, the case of the widespread vilification in Mexico of the Hollywood star Lupe Vélez, whose Latina persona in films of the 1930s and 1940s revealed the precariousness of the solidity and stability of Mexican identity and the threat posed to that identity by the growing exodus of citizens to the north (Fregoso 112). Mexican films dealing with the border are, according to Fojas, strongly nationalist and dismissive of the "American Dream" (4–5). In general terms, however, exchanges of various types have abounded between the two national cinemas, making the border truly porous in filmic terms: from individual agreements between the two countries—such as the one at Estudios Churubusco in the 1940s, which turned the Mexican film company into the locus of transnational and state-to-state collaboration (Fein 85)—to the hybrid national identity of such icons of Mexican cinema as Dolores del Río and Pedro Armendáriz.

More specifically, the Mexico–U.S. border has produced the border film, a rich genre with a long history in both countries. Writing in 1990, David R. Maciel analyzes a large number of films, both Mexican and U.S. American, from the 1970s and 1980s and laments the scarcity of positive and/or complex representations of life in *la frontera* in them, finding a glimmer of hope in the independent cinema of the United States (84). More recently, Camilla Fojas has returned to the genre, concentrating almost exclusively on U.S. productions as "the most pervasive image machine of the border region for a global industry" (3). For her, the U.S. genre is not generally about the immigrant experience or about cultural conflict but rather about the reassertion and fortification of U.S. national identity, even though some recent films, including *Lone Star* (1996), *The Three Burials of Melquiades Estrada*, and *Babel*, have brought to light much that had been repressed, like the importance of the Mexican in the genesis of southwestern culture (11). Whether independent or mainstream, the genre continues to flourish, not only in Hollywood but also in Mexican cinema, as well as in the growing number of coproductions between the two countries like *A Day without a Mexican* (2004), *Under the Same Moon* (2007), and, of course, *Babel*. Many of these films focus on the generally dramatic experience of the *mojados,* the illegal border-crossers searching for a better life "al otro lado" and finding various disappointments, from the critically acclaimed independent U.S. films Robert Young's *Alambrista!* (1977) and Gregory Nava's *El Norte* (1983) to recent documentaries like *Mojados, into the Night* (2004) or fictional films like *Fast Food Nation.*

Conversely, going against the grain of traditional Mexican discourses on border crossings, some contemporary Mexican movies, like *El agujero* (The Hole; 1997) and *De ida y vuelta* (Back and forth; 2000), reflect the frustrations of returning emigrants whose fantasies of an idealized homeland do not correspond to the reality they find when they get there. At the end of *De ida y vuelta,* its protagonist, fed up with all sorts of mishaps and indignities, decides to go back to the other side. Still, movie characters, like thousands of real people year after year, continue to undertake the journey, including children who cross borders to look for their parents in the three stories of *Al otro lado* and the crowd-pleaser

Under the Same Moon. Wish-fulfillment can also take the form of comic satire, as in the celebratory ending of Cheech Marin's *Born in East L.A.* (1987), in which a U.S. citizen of Mexican origin, Rudy (Marin), helps dozens of illegal immigrants get into his country after undergoing the humiliation of mistaken deportation. These and many other border films conceive the experience of the border on a vertical axis; that is, they explore, although hardly ever exclusively, *la frontera* as a line to be crossed, an obstacle to be overcome, in the context of a journey to the north and sometimes the south: at the beginning of María Novaro's *Sin dejar huella*, for example, a character crosses through a hole in the fence to Ciudad Juárez and starts a journey that will take her south to Cancún. Other border films emphasize the horizontal axis of their stories, representing not one but multiple and more or less habitual crossings as well as life along the border. *Born in East L.A.* begins and ends with two crossings, but for much of its story it places its protagonist in Tijuana and traces his process of adaptation to an alien border culture. Tijuana is also the location of Novaro's *El jardín del Edén*, in which three women cross their lives and journeys and interact in various ways in the border town. As in the Cheech Marin film, the protagonists of Gregory Nava's *Mi familia/My Family* (1995) are citizens of East Los Angeles, and the film explores the stories of successive generations of Chicanos and the changing conditions of life in the course of several decades in a city that is revealed to possess a rich border culture that hundreds of Hollywood films had systematically ignored before. In a different register, *A Day without a Mexican* turns this invisibility into the engine of its comic fantasy and imagines what would happen in the United States if people of Mexican origin were to suddenly disappear. Nava's next film, the biopic *Selena* (1997), about the successful Tejana pop singer who was killed at an early age by the president of her fan club, also focuses on life on *la frontera*, this time the Texan border, highlighting, as in the case of Tin-Tan's films, the positive aspects of hybrid identity.

The Texan border as seen from a U.S. perspective has also been the subject of numerous films, including recent ones like John Sayles's *Lone Star*, Nava's *Bordertown* (2006), the Coen brothers' *No Country for Old Men* (2007), and *The Three Burials of Melquiades Estrada*. In spite of occasional criticism of its ideological project (Fregoso 56),

Sayles's movie excels at delineating the complexity and fluidity of life north of the border and the long history of various types of exchanges between races and ethnic groups in the significantly named Texas town of Frontera. Telling a series of parallel stories of Anglos and Mexicans, parents and children, past and present, it uses the narrative incident of unexpected blood relations as a metaphor of the unique mongrel texture of the region and the many layers it discloses once we start delving. More simplistically, *No Country for Old Men* sets its meditation on the senseless absurdity of a contemporary world beset by violence on the Mexico–U.S. border because of the contemporary associations of the region with drug traffic, whereas *Bordertown* explores violence on the other side, dramatizing through the generic conventions of the mainstream thriller the story of the many Mexican women mysteriously murdered in Ciudad Juárez in the 1990s (see Fregoso 6–8).

In recent decades, academic writing has called attention to the region north of the border—its long, largely untold history of oppression of one culture by another, and the increasingly visible artistic manifestations of a rich and sophisticated culture in literature, painting, popular music, and other arts, including film. By contrast, the southern part of that region has remained relatively unexplored by U.S. and Mexican cinema, with only occasional narratives that zero in on the excesses and exploitation of the *maquiladora* industry, as in the case of *Bordertown* and documentaries like *Maquilapolis* (2006). This horizontal axis of cinematic representation, focusing on those who inhabit the borderland permanently and whose identity is closely linked to that experience, continues to grow in size and diversity, as the presence of Mexicans and people of Mexican origin becomes more visible throughout the United States. *Real Women Have Curves* (2002) and *Quinceañera* (2006), for example, tell stories about a city of Los Angeles that looks very different from traditional cinematic representations, in which Chicano teenagers, poised, as is often the case, between two cultures, are seen in an unstoppable process of redefining identity and, by so doing, changing the shape of the ever-expanding borderland.

The distinctiveness of *The Three Burials of Melquiades Estrada* within the panorama briefly sketched above lies in its consecutive representation of the horizontal and the vertical axes, bringing together two types of border stories in a single narrative. Arriaga employs the multiprotagonist, scrambled-narrative template to show a slice of border life in Texas in the first third of the film, focusing mostly on Anglo characters, and then the story changes drastically, becoming a road movie, as three of the characters (two alive, one dead) undertake a difficult journey across the border to Melquiades's birthplace. Both *la frontera* as an area and a cultural concept and the cross-border journey are successively highlighted by a text that simultaneously encapsulates the two cultural dimensions of border representations. Many border movies share elements of both axes, but *Melquiades* probably visualizes this generic bifurcation most clearly, turning it into the driving force of its structure. *Babel* continues this exploration of the possibilities of the genre but goes one step further. It incorporates itself within the ever-growing corpus of the border film with a story that features a return journey from the United States to Mexico and a snatch of life on the southern side of the San Ysidro border. At the same time, *Babel* frames its border story within a much larger canvas that encompasses various reverberations of the concept of *la frontera* in contemporary life, a strategy made possible through the combination of two genres: the border movie and the multiprotagonist film.

Bienvenida a Tijuana

In the Amelia story of *Babel*, we see the characters cross the border twice, but the experience is very different depending on the direction of the crossing. Going into Mexico, the text focuses on the point of view of the children, who have never been across before and for whom everything is new and exciting. In an approximately two-minute sequence, the film packs sixty-four shots that alternate between the young people's expressions of curiosity and anticipation looking through the windows of Santiago's car and images of Tijuana full of color, movement, and energy (fig. 21). The song "Cumbia sobre el río," which can be heard over this montage sequence, becomes for the children and the spectators a musical greeting to the southern country. The crossing is perceived as a joyful experience, a fit prelude to the wedding celebration. At one point, Santiago rhetorically asks Debbie and Mike, "See how easy it is to come into paradise?" There is nobody to stop them at the line dividing the two countries, and their passage is free and straightforward. "Paradise" includes such warnings of its ambivalence as a road sign just before they

Figure 21. Bienvenida a Tijuana: *Babel.* I

get to the border of a family of three running with the caption "wanted" above them, or several shots of the fence with crosses hanging from it. Yet the overall impression—created through fast cutting, constant movement inside the frame, and the gay music—is of relentless energy and exhilaration. Tijuana is the most unambiguously positive space in *Babel,* the closest one can get to paradise in a movie about transnational stories, intercultural communication, and borders of various kinds.

Returning in the middle of the following night through the Tecate pass, the situation is very different for the same characters. The sequence is much longer (almost six minutes), the cutting pattern is more irregular and nervous, the music (which has been prominent throughout the scenes of the Tijuana plot) has disappeared, and the overwhelming impression of color in the bright morning is now replaced by the monotonous, dark-bluish tones of the night. The emphasis is no longer on the excitement of crossing to the other side but rather on the imperviousness of a border that has suddenly lost much of its porosity and has enlarged the distance between the two adjoining countries. Most of the scene is taken up by the tense conversation between a drunken and increasingly irritated Santiago and a routinely suspicious border officer, with Amelia looking on with an expression of growing worry on her face. The handheld camera shakes and wobbles as it tightly frames the characters in claustrophobic short distances, figuring the border as a cage from which it is difficult to break free rather than as the gate to a new world, and anticipating Santiago's decision to drive into the United States without authorization.

Regardless of the specific behavior of the characters involved in this incident, the text calls attention to the contrast between the two sequences, a contrast that becomes part of the film's ideology. Within the narrative structure, this disparity is enhanced by their aftermaths: the brief journey south is followed by the celebratory mood of a wedding party; the second border crossing ends with Amelia and the children stranded in the desert. The two experiences are further contextualized by the parallel event in Morocco: while Amelia, the children's "substitute" mother, is deported as a consequence of the incident, never to see the children whom she loves again, their real mother is evacuated to a hospital in Casablanca by a U.S. helicopter, the accidental shot that wounded her almost causing a diplomatic crisis between the two countries. Those protected from the other by borders are protected wherever they go, or whatever their attitude; those rejected by them are soon forgotten.

Since its beginnings in the 1980s, border theory has explored the cultural and political causes that produce such differences and asymmetries as well as the growing variety and complexity of border experience and its representation in cultural texts. In her seminal work *Borderlands/La Frontera: The New Mestiza* (1999), Gloria Anzaldúa theorizes the border on two levels. Borders are "set up to define the places that are safe and unsafe, to distinguish *us* from *them*. A border is a dividing line, a narrow strip along a steep edge" (25). This accurately describes the Tecate border crossing in *Babel,* where the border police are deployed and briefed to ensure the safety of the territory they are guarding—in this case, the United States. This strategy may or may not guarantee the searched-for protection, but it also turns the border, as we see in the film, into a space of repression, injustice, and suffering for those who are not protected by it. Elsewhere, however, Anzaldúa offers a different dimension of the concept: "The borderlands are physically present whenever two or more cultures edge on each other, where people of different races occupy the same territory, where under, lower, middle and upper classes touch, where the space between two individuals shrinks with intimacy" (19). This second definition has proved crucial to expand the consideration of borders beyond the materiality of dividing lines and fences across the world, allowing for more metaphorical representations such as the ones that we can see in the rest of the stories in *Babel*. At the same time, without straying too far from the material borders, the definition expands the term in a different direction: from border to borderland. The new concept encompasses not only dividing lines, wires, or fences but the territories around them, where, on the one hand, different cultures and identities are constantly put into contact and, on the other hand, a specific type of identity, border identity, is developed. While the Tecate border episode illustrates the limiting perspective of the border as a line to be (or not to be) crossed, the earlier crossing and the rest of the story expand that line to a wider territory. The emphasis on the children's point of view reveals the border as a fruitful place of exchange, although one in which potential or real conflict is never far away.

In a world characterized by more frequent and intense transnational links between people, the border is where the transnational takes place, and the borderland is the space constructed around such exchanges. Noticing the power of the concept to describe a contemporary condition that extends well beyond the material borders between countries, other authors have called attention to the significance of the space of the borderland, with definitions such as "contact zones" (Pratt 6) or "cultural force fields" (Carolyn Porter qtd. in Benito and Manzanas 4). These are spaces in which cultures "edge on each other," to repeat Anzaldúa's words, or, in Iñárritu's equally forceful description, "where the most noble dreams overlap with the saddest ends" (García 257). In cultural theory, the border has become, therefore, a line of exclusion and conflict, of paranoid defence against the other, and a space of integration and hybridity, a meeting point between cultures, where different groups clash but also enrich each other and form the mongrel identity that, to a large extent, characterizes contemporary society. As Benito and Manzanas argue, the border repeats and diversifies itself in different locations and times (4). In a world defined by multiple migrations, it flares up wherever two people or groups of people from different cultural origins are thrown together or next to one another, which can happen very far away from geographical borders. Films like *The Visitor* (2008) or *Gran Torino* (2008) place such border encounters far away from material lines between countries, in the middle of Manhattan and in a working-class suburb of Detroit, respectively.

However, when we think about borders in more or less metaphorical ways and are tempted to wax lyrical about their cultural potential, we must not lose sight of their materiality and the multiple realities of suffering, oppression, and injustice they constantly generate. Asked in a 1980s interview about the academic popularity of the concept, the writer and scholar Norma Elia Cantú replied: "What bothers me sometimes is people who come to use the word 'border' without any realization of the very real geopolitical space where people are dying. There's no *conciencia* about that real political situation, and it becomes something theoretical and abstract, disconnected from that reality." For Camilla Fojas, too many Hollywood border films represent peaceful interracial and international relations that deny the sociocultural realities and tensions of the borderland. She follows Pablo Vila in arguing that the border is more "a place of conflict and contention than of cohesion and confluence" (Fojas 13). *Babel* encourages us to expand our perspective on borders well beyond the lines of separation between countries and the spaces created around them and warns against a perspective that forgets that, beyond theoretical conceptualizations, borders continue to be specific geographical places where experiences like Amelia's take place every day. Borderlands are fraught spaces where contact can easily turn into friction and confrontation, and traumatic experiences are probably more frequent than uplifting ones. An analysis of the importance of the border and the borderland in Iñárritu's film must therefore start with its representation of the "real" border between the United States and Mexico.

Echoing the warnings of cultural critics, *Babel* is highly ambivalent about its representation of the borderland: while the Tijuana scenes are mostly celebratory of the exuberance of south-of-the-border culture, the story is peppered with ambiguous narrative elements, from Mike's shock at the killing of the chicken to the whole construction of Santiago's character. This ambivalence is basic to understanding the role played by Tijuana as a real place and symbolic space in the movie. In *Babel*, the old harbor of San Diego becomes the center of the borderland, with the U.S. city as an appendage, overturning for once the geopolitical hierarchy. The picture of Tijuana in Iñárritu's film departs from the usual connotations of sordidness, poverty, and danger that even films like *El jardín del Edén* or *Born in East L.A.* evoke, an image that is consistently furthered by press coverage abroad. Moving beyond earlier representations, it attempts to capture the city's geographical and historical uniqueness. In an article on Tijuana, Néstor García Canclini describes it as one of the greatest laboratories of postmodernity, a city with a strong personality defined by border life and intercultural contacts (*Culturas* 286), where definitions of identity and culture are reelaborated on the basis of border experience (294). There is, at the same time, a certain tension in what he perceives as the peculiarity of Tijuana identity. On the one hand, the Tijuanenses define themselves through border life and intercultural exchanges and see their city as a space in a state of permanent reinvention, where borders fall and are reerected every day, where nothing is real but simulacra: from the false zebras to the illegal emigrants. On the other hand, these same people insist on fixing signs of identification and rituals that distinguish them from those in transit to another place (293–95). This is a city where roots are desired and despised, where place identity is strongly marked and fragile, where people are from nowhere in particular yet soon become oddly attached to this no-man's-land.

The pop song "Bienvenida a Tijuana," by the Franco-Spanish singer Manu Chao, is one of many recent manifestations of border culture that can be linked to the Amelia story of *Babel* in successfully capturing the city's volatile and paradoxical character. Sung in mongrelized Spanish or English, depending on the version, it blends a variety of musical styles to convey the idea of a transitional space. Chao, the epitome of the contemporary transnational artist, represents Tijuana, like Canclini, as a contradictory place that welcomes those who are in transit to what they hope will be a better life and those for whom San Diego has become an impossible dream and offers them an alternative world in the hope that they may find it more attractive and stay, at least for a while. The lyrics evoke the drama of immigration and diaspora but turn the well-known reality of Mexican and Latin American immigration into a celebration and a vindication of "la raza de la frontera," a group identity that appeals to the experience of millions of people in contemporary societies. They reflect the growing social relevance of "diasporic public spheres," the term Arjun Appadurai coined at the end of the twentieth century to describe the most formidable challenge to the increasingly questionable myths of origin promoted by traditional national identities (10).

Chao's performance of the song in different versions and musical genres all around the world extends the symbolism of Tijuana beyond its complex geographical location, but conversely, the singer's presence in the border town at the beginning of the twenty-first century, along with that of other popular artists, reinforced the peculiarity of border culture. Josh Kun looks at the meanings of a group that emerged from this particular background, Tijuana NO!, a band that is not nationally constructed and that defines itself as a border phenomenon with a highly ambivalent relationship to both Mexico and the United States. According to Kun, Tijuana NO!, with its aggressive attacks on economic and political institutions on both sides of the border, questions definitions of the local and the global, the national and the transnational, and demands a new grammar of globalization (108). Beyond the specific political agenda or generic conventions employed by the individual artists, the significance of Tijuana lies in the specificity of its diasporic identity: an urban monster built around movement and impermanence, a visible embodiment of such an intangible concept as the space of flows.

Kun evokes May Joseph's term "nomadic citizenship"—a citizenship that is performed both across and within national boundaries (109) or, we would argue, a citizenship that springs from the boundary itself—to define Tijuana NO! This third country, a concept that Anzaldúa adapts from Homi Bhabha's hybrid space (25), rejects the nation-state yet would not exist without it. It finds in Tijuana both a physical embodiment and a cultural icon: in elevating the experience of migrating, of passing through, to the core element of modern identity, it imagines a new space that is superimposed on geopolitical separations and therefore depends on them but at the same time erases and transcends them in order to construct the paradoxical home of the nomadic citizen.

A more traditional and mainstream group of *corridos norteños,* Los Tigres del Norte, has been drawing over the years the blueprint of this third country through their numerous and often controversial songs, characterized again by the trope of the crossing, whether by drug traffickers, *mojados,* corrupt capitalists, or other nomadic citizens. In their lyrics, Jalisco, Acapulco, San Francisco, Chicago, Oregon, New York, and even Madrid and Rome belong to the common space of the borderland, the elastic and mutant space on which border identity is reaffirmed every day. Whether critical, celebratory, or, as is often the case, merely descriptive, the fictional world created by this band both rejects the exclusionary dimension of the border and exists as a consequence of its reality. Cultural texts like Los Tigres del Norte's texts, Chao's song, or Iñárritu's third feature reveal a thickening of the thin line and the creation of an increasingly rich and habitable space as a result of that thickening.

In *Babel*, Tijuana is the site of the diasporic public sphere and Amelia the nomadic citizen, not so much because she is constantly on the move but because her three journeys across the border and the two spaces that she inhabits in the film—the San Diego house and the village where her son is getting married—are defined by her hybrid identity. More than any other character or narrative element, she embodies the complexities and contradictions of the border as borderland. She is an icon of the "meXicana" theorized by Rosa Linda Fregoso as an interface between *mexicana* and *chicana,* a woman who seems equally at home on both sides of the border and facilitates exchanges between communities and identities, as well as embodying the vulnerability and suffering associated with everyday border experience. She is also the new type of cultural citizen produced by the borderlands (xiv–xv), an inhabitant of the third country. At the same time, she is presented from the beginning as the compliant victim of social oppression and, in the story's *dénouement,* of the inequalities produced by the reinforcement of borders, persistent national identities, and widespread arrogance and intolerance. In *Babel*, Amelia's identity is closely linked to that of Tijuana as a border area. She presides over the joyful experience of Tijuana as "paradise" for the children but also becomes the victim of border exclusion.

The opening scene of her story, in the San Diego house, in which she plays hide-and-seek with her two charges before putting them to bed, is visually characterized by a similar ambivalence. As in his first two films, Iñárritu creates here a sense of space that is closely linked to the textual signifying structure through formal means—in this case, a particular use of the mise-en-scène. The filmmakers have explained that they used the color red as a central motif throughout the film to unify the four different stories and the three locations and then played with variations depending on the episode: umber for Morocco, primary red for Mexico, and pink/magenta for Tokyo (Bosley 1). Within each of the segments, however, further variation is frequent. In this scene, the red of Amelia's t-shirt combines with other objects of the same color in the kitchen, living room, and children's bedroom, with the brown of walls and cupboards, and with the warm artificial lighting to compose a rich atmosphere in which spectators can vividly share in the feeling of protection and well-being that emanates from the protagonist and is directed toward the children. The house is constructed as an enclosed space, a safe environment in which nothing bad could possibly happen to the children. The walls of the San Diego house can be seen as a metaphor for Amelia's attitude toward Mike and Debbie, evoking the role of borders in keeping us from external danger.

Moreover, in a film that deals with the many facets of borders, these walls mirror the fence that the children will soon see when they are about to cross into Mexico. This notorious wall, which the U.S. government began building in the 1990s as a way to keep the *mojados* out, has become, in Iñárritu's words, "the greatest monument to intolerance in human history" (*Babel* press kit 18). Yet it is also part of the landscape of this particular borderland, a prop used by children to play games on the Tijuana beach or by their parents to protect themselves from the sun. Near the spot where the fence, rather absurdly, goes into the Pacific Ocean in an apparent attempt to separate U.S. from Mexican water particles, an old milestone marks the spot where in the past one could stand simultaneously on the two countries and reenact the meeting of cultures, a celebration made impossible by the adjoining wall. The juxtaposition of both objects as contradictory markers of the line becomes a poignant embodiment of the ambivalence of the borderland. García Canclini contended that the wire separating Mexico from the United States could be seen as the main monument of border culture (*Culturas* 292). Now the wire has been replaced by a fence, but it continues to accrue ambivalent and complex meanings.

In integrating the wall and all the tragic stories that are grafted onto it as part of the exciting first-time cross-border experience, *Babel* once again reverses its connotations and incorporates it into the landscape of the borderland, defying its divisive nature and redefining it as a symbol of a new culture, a celebration of the porosity it denies but cannot prevent. The San Diego house, with its prominent walls and demarcating lines, suggests the same contradictory meanings. Safeguarding the children from the various threats of the border town, encapsulated in their mother's teaching that Mexico is a dangerous country, the house is presided over by the undocumented immigrant, a representative of those dangers, who has paradoxically become a guardian angel for Mike and Debbie. The primary red of Amelia's t-shirt and of the objects around her emphasizes her Mexicanness, producing another reversal whereby the threatening other becomes the agent of safety. This safety, however, does not extend to Amelia herself, and the film also visualizes this contradiction in this scene, anticipating future events: when Richard telephones from Morocco, the camera frames her as constrained by the vertical lines of the walls and the horizontal lines, top and bottom, of the kitchen cupboards (fig. 22). The protective space suddenly becomes a repressive space that cuts her head off from visibility and limits her movements. Amelia is therefore both nurturer and victim of this metaphoric borderland, upholder of the inviolability of national identity and intruder to be gotten rid of, depending on framing and camera perspective.

The "silent invasion" is given an ironic reversal the next morning by Santiago's noisy arrival. Amelia's red t-shirt has now been replaced by a blue jacket as she gets more and more caught up in the problems caused by the children's parents' absence. This change to blue is an anticipation

Figure 22. Protective and repressive space:
Amelia in *Babel*.

of the dominant color in the return border scene as a consequence of which she will be finally deported, but rather than a complete substitution, what we perceive now is a combination of both colors. Among the numerous visible signifiers of Mexico contained in Santiago's car is a red sticker of the Virgen de Guadalupe in the rear window. When Mike goes into the back seat, he looks around and sees Amelia framed by the sticker, identifying her with the most famous symbol of Mexican femininity (fig. 23), the good mother described by Anzaldúa in the following terms: "Today, *la Virgen de Guadalupe* is the single most potent religious, political and cultural image of the Chicano/*mexicano*. She, like my race, is a synthesis of the old world and the new, of the religion and culture of the two races in our psyche, the conquerors and the conquered. She is the symbol of the *mestizo* true to his or her Indian values" (52). From Mike's viewpoint, Amelia is also the good mother, also defined by her *mestizo* identity, who, through her caring influence, may make him and his sister inhabitants of the same borderland, future hybrid citizens in spite of the color of their skin. At the same time, the juxtaposition of red and blue defines the two dimensions of Amelia as a character: her "red" identity as both Mexican and meXicana, a nomadic citizen of the borderland, and her "blue" social position as an undocumented immigrant in a society that uses her and rejects her.

Figure 23. Amelia as a modern-day
Virgen de Guadalupe in *Babel*.

For the film, however, she continues to be the emotional and moral center of the Tijuana narrative. She embodies the space of the border, which shrinks to the size of an Anglo house in San Diego or expands to the dusty site of a wedding celebration across the line depending on her presence. In San Diego she is defined by her relationship with her young charges, but once she crosses the border, other dimensions of her identity become apparent. The montage sequence of the borderland as a new world for Mike and Debbie briefly transfers the focus from Amelia to the space for which she stands, but as soon as she arrives at her own children's house, and the deep red of her party dress is festively mirrored in the outfits of the *norteño* band hired for the occasion, in the plastic chairs and tables, and in the various shades of other characters' clothes, she takes center stage again.

One of the most characteristic scenes of this section is the last time we see the group at the party before they drive back to the border. In a film in which the musical sound track plays a crucial role, this scene is dominated by Chavela Vargas's melancholy song "Tú me acostumbraste." The famous singer's characteristic slow and broken delivery is matched by the slight slow motion of the images—according to Iñárritu, the scene was shot at thirty frames per second (García 258)—giving the action a mesmeric quality and elevating the dancing, drinking, and mayhem of late-night partying to an ambivalent exploration of Amelia's *mestiza* identity. As she dances with her son and, inside the house, passionately kisses a friend from her Mexican past, the lively *corrido* music of the band is replaced by the love ballad, equally characteristic of Mexican culture but very different in terms of register and cultural connotations. Amelia stands between the two of them, equally at home with their respective musical styles, as she is shown to be equally at home on both sides of the border and with her two sets of "children." The slow motion follows the rhythm of the ballad and defamiliarizes the images, lifting them out of their realistic context and asking us to see the wedding party as a denationalized metaphor for the third country and Amelia as its most privileged inhabitant, the queen of this diasporic kingdom whose red dress represents its energy and its suffering. While the images are visually manipulated and powerfully influenced by Vargas's distinctive voice, Adriana Barraza's compelling performance realistically conveys the humility and the tendency to make herself invisible that also characterizes Iñárritu's view of the immigrant woman. The rootedness of the performance and of the geographical and cultural location of the party contrasts, therefore, with the nomadic nature of Amelia's identity and the defamiliarized and mixed character of the representation. Her kingdom continues to be as elusive as the national identities from which it feeds continue to be deep-seated. The love song is reframed as a hymn to intercultural communication, a celebration of the citizen of the borderland. However, the sense of loss contained in the lyrics looks forward not so much to the character's loss in being deported from the place where she has lived for the last fourteen years as to our own loss in a world that will be much poorer without her.

The shallow focus that is used in many of the shots of this scene, separating the characters from the blurred background and increasing its hypnotic quality, can also be seen as an anticipation of the two shots that close the final segment of Amelia's story. After being deported from the United States, she returns to Tijuana, where her son comes to meet her and lovingly embraces her at the outset of her new life (fig. 24). Tijuana, the capital of the borderland kingdom, momentarily disappears from view to make the spectator focus, as in 21 *Grams*, on the exchange of emotions between the characters. But, in a different sense, the use of out-of-focus lifts the city from its geographical location and turns it

Figure 24. Tijuana as cultural borderland:
Amelia and Luis embrace in *Babel*.

into an abstract symbol of the cultural borderland, revealing its function as a literal contact zone, where, to repeat Anzaldúa's words, the space between people, countries, and cultures shrinks with intimacy. Whereas our first contact with Tijuana took place in the spectacular montage sequence of the first border crossing and was characterized by the visibility of the immediately recognizable signs of its border identity, in these last shots the city appears to dissolve behind the characters, pointing at the other identity of the borderland: the "empty" space where exchanges, negotiations, and flows between people take place. In evolving in this direction, Tijuana also points to the film's overarching approach to the deployment of space, an approach that reproduces Castells's dichotomy of a space of places and a space of flows and situates *Babel* within the boundaries of contemporary transnational culture.

The Transitional and the Transnational

In isolating the characters from the background at certain points, *Babel* resembles *21 Grams;* but as a whole, its attitude toward space is radically different. Even more than in *Amores perros,* Iñárritu's third film gives us a vivid sense of locatedness: the physical space of Tokyo, the Moroccan villages, and the U.S.–Mexican border at times take center stage and appear to be more important than the characters. In the Amelia story, a balance is struck between space and character, between the borderland and the protagonist, both closely linked as part of the same cultural phenomenon. Something similar happens with the rest of the locations. Medium shots can be found in the movie, but its preferred camera distances are the close-up and extreme close-up, on the one hand, and the long shot and the extreme long shot, on the other hand. Various formal strategies are deployed to make the landscapes and cityscapes distinctive, visually spectacular, and narratively central.

At the same time, the multiprotagonist structure creates a different space, one that accurately represents the experience of living in contemporary globalized, transnational societies. In this respect, the transitions between scenes are particularly meaningful points in the film's formal and thematic structure. It could be argued that these transitions are the cinematic equivalent of border crossings and that in *Babel* editing between narrative blocks becomes a formal correlative of the network society as theorized by Manuel Castells. The space thus constructed reproduces in narrative form a pattern of social communication revolving around places (geographical locations) and flows (links of various kinds between those locations, interactions between social actors). Through his formal and narrative choices in this film, Iñárritu suggests that both types of space are equally crucial to understanding our world and that neither could exist without the other. Castells argues that in our time, places are becoming disembodied from their cultural, historical, and geographical meaning and reintegrated into functional networks, the space of flows substituting for the space of places (406). In *Babel*, the lives of characters are centrally affected by transnational interactions and flows. Their place identity becomes all the more porous and fragile because of this process, but their physical context is still very much part of what they are. In some cases, as we have just seen with Amelia, the space that defines them and the space that they construct with their identity is not merely a combination of flows and places but one that is simultaneously both: the borderland.

From the materiality of the border and the cultural relevance of the borderland as they are explored in the Tijuana section of *Babel,* Iñárritu expands the meaning of those concepts through a proliferation of stories that reflect a contemporary world constantly crossed by real and metaphorical borders. The director has repeatedly explained that the real borders are not external physical lines but are inside us—they are fences between ideas (Iñárritu, *Babel* press kit 4). Although the Tijuana story proves that he never underestimates the importance of those physical lines, the film as a whole relocates those lines to the space between individuals, whether they share a contiguous physical place or are linked through the space of flows. But, as with the Mexico–U.S. borderland, these lines are not only obstacles, exclusionary strategies, and bearers of potential conflict; they also facilitate communication, exchanges, and feelings between people. In fact, both the space of places and the space of flows, both strategies of mise-en-scène and editing, make communication inevitable, although never easy. The biblical story of Babel becomes not only a metaphor for those things that separate and alienate people but also for the human impulse that brought them together in the first place and, in spite of the difficulties created by the divine punishment of different languages, will continue to bring them together.

A transnational, borderland space is constructed both within each of the twenty-four narrative blocks that make up the film's structure and in the twenty-three transitions between them. Amelia's border identity originates from her experience as a "nomadic citizen." In one of the stories in Morocco, Richard and Susan's stay in Tazarine brings them into contact with a different culture in a way that they had not experienced in their much closer relationship with Amelia's "otherness" and also turns them into citizens of a transnational space. The brothers Ahmed and Yussef and their family only see the other from far away, but Ahmed's rifle shot constitutes an unexpected intercultural link that shows a different side of transnational intercommunication and brings them tragic consequences. Within the Chieko story, borders are mostly of the internal and metaphorical kind mentioned by Iñárritu, and hints of the characters' existence in a network society appear in more indirect ways. At the same time, the transitions detach the characters from their geographical context and deterritorialize space, multiplying links between the stories, suggesting an increasing number of ramifications of the individual plots, and evoking an experience that, in some cases, is at odds with the physical or psychological remoteness of the characters and their place identity. This web is reinforced by an intricate use of music in the sound track.

The first transition in the film bridges the story of Yussef and Ahmed and the scene in the San Diego house analyzed above. Yussef has just shot at the bus from the hilltop, where he is practicing with their father's new rifle. A few seconds later the bus stops. The children realize that something has happened, and they start running away. On the cut, their movement segues into Mike running in his house in California, playing hide-and-seek with Amelia and his sister (figs. 25–26). The sequence feels almost like a match on action or even a jump cut and, for a split second, the inattentive spectator may assume that it is indeed the same movement with the same characters. We soon realize, however, that the background has changed from outdoors to indoors, the colors have changed within the film's general red pattern, and those running are different children. We immediately understand that there has been a change of scene and narrative block and that the film has moved from the story of the Moroccan family to that of the San Diego–Tijuana border, inaugurating a pattern of transitions between blocks that will not change until the end of the movie. This false jump cut establishes continuity

Figures 25–26. Let the children play:
transnational transitions in *Babel*.

between two stories, two spaces, and two sets of characters that are separated by thousands of miles. Once continuity has been ascertained, the differences and contrasts between the two adjoining shots and the two scenes become increasingly obvious.

The two pairs of children, Yussef and Ahmed and Mike and Debbie, remain separate in their two stories and are never directly linked by the narrative, except for the fact that the person Yussef has just inadvertently shot happens to be the U.S. children's mother. Yet the visual link between them suggests connections of various kinds and invites spectators to speculate about them. To start with, both sets of children are playing games, as children ought to do, and we are encouraged to see the dramatic and snowballing consequences of the Moroccan children's game as a consequence of the geopolitical situation that makes the environments in which both pairs of children are growing up so drastically different. We saw in the previous section how the safety of Debbie and Mike's home is predicated on the vulnerability of the person who provides the protective atmosphere. By extension, in a more abstract sense it is also dependent on Yussef and Ahmed's defenselessness. The color structure of the film further joins the two actions through the common red spectrum, while at the same time emphasizing the obvious differences: the Moroccan children are outdoors, surrounded by the hostile, mountainous environment, while the other two are safely indoors, protected by the pure reds and browns of the family home.

The ideological statement implicit in this visual transition is given a more immediate, historically specific explanation: as a consequence of the September 11 terrorist attacks, border-protection policy was strengthened in the United States, including the Mexican border, and immigration legislation was toughened and more strictly enforced. Amelia's summary deportation may be seen as a direct consequence of this historical background. The other obvious consequence was that any incident involving Western and especially U.S. citizens in Arab countries became immediately branded as a terrorist attack, which is precisely the interpretation that Susan's shooting is given by the diplomatic authorities. Amelia and the Moroccan children and their family are innocent victims of historical circumstances that are closely linked, in spite of the distance between them, and they are both related to the safety and protection of the members of the same U.S. family. In any case, the transition partakes of a pattern, typical of multiprotagonist films, whereby different storylines are not to be understood and interpreted in isolation but in their relation to one another. Even when the stories appear, as in much of *Babel*, to be independent of one another, each becomes part of the signifying pattern of the rest. The visual continuity established in the transitional cuts points to the manner in which the multiprotagonist plot should be read, while at the same time underlining the differences between the events that are formally linked. As in the two earlier movies, we are simultaneously aware of the intricate web that joins human beings in contemporary societies and of the radical differences among them.

As the narrative develops, the transitions become particularly intense points around which meanings multiply. However, the patterns of integration between the different geographical places are not necessarily symmetrical. Among the four stories, the Chieko one is the most distant in narrative terms. The connection between its plot and those of the others remains hidden for a relatively long time, and even when we do find out that the rifle with which Yussef has shot Susan is the same rifle that Chieko's father had given his guide as a goodbye present when he was in Morocco the previous year, the link remains weak. Accordingly, the early transitions to and from the Tokyo story may emphasize contrasts rather than continuities. One such transition, for example, connects Susan's shrieking in Tazarine when the Moroccan vet is stitching her wound with a dentist's receptionist in Tokyo mouthing inaudible words. The next shot reveals that this is Chieko's perspective, the shot of the receptionist reflecting her perception of reality. The disparity between the two shots is enhanced by the frantic motion of the former and the stasis of the latter, and by the contrast between relative darkness in Morocco and uniform light at the dentist's clinic in Tokyo. This cut appears to keep the two episodes apart visually, yet the contrast also alerts us to the fact that both scenes narrate instances of women suffering acutely, in one case physically, in the other psychologically.

Once the transitions have been established as important narrative elements and the spectator has learned to appreciate their ability to join episodes, connections automatically proliferate, even when they are not as explicit as those underlined by continuity. A later transition between these two episodes links Richard's desolation and feeling of guilt at failing his wife once again with a detail shot of Chieko's mother's photo on a mantelpiece in her apartment. The thematic connection here is between two husbands: Richard, estranged from a wife who could be dying because of his decisions; and Yasujiro, whose wife killed herself in despair, although the film never explains her reasons. Additionally, while Susan's suffering had already been related to Chieko's, it is now Richard's anguish that is linked to the pain felt by the Japanese teenager, since once again the shot of her mother's portrait is immediately revealed to be framed from her point of view. At this point, with the spectator well accustomed to the rich web of connotations suggested by the transitions, we may, for example, speculate that Chieko's present spiritual crisis is the consequence of what happened between her parents in the past, an obviously troubled relationship that is now mirrored in the growing gulf between Susan and Richard. While the visual links between narrative blocks are sometimes more obvious than others, once the meaning-making potential of the transitions has been triggered, there is no stopping the multiple-connection game.

Openly political statements of the type mentioned above are inevitable in a story that connects developed with developing regions around the world, but the film seems to be more interested in how the network society affects individuals. Political power and powerlessness are never far from the characters' circumstances, but *Babel* is truly interested in the bottom-up power theorized by Michel Foucault, the power relations that automatically appear whenever two people relate to one another in any sort of situation (92–97). However, for Iñárritu, interpersonal relationships are not only defined by power but also by the deep urge to reach out for the other and by the vulnerability and brevity of affection. For this reason, transitions in *Babel* are largely focused on individual characters and how their plights are reflected in and/or affected by those of other characters in often distant spaces.

False jump cuts and visual contrasts are not the only formal strategies employed to connect characters and spaces at transitional points. Other techniques associated with classical continuity also suggest realistically impossible connections: we seem to see the tourists in Morocco from the point of view of Santiago as he gets into his car to drive to Tijuana; or, when they are already in Tijuana, Mike looks in horror at a chicken being killed, but the final shot of the narrative block, a medium shot of the child looking offscreen left, is followed, in another false eyeline match, by his mother inside the bus just after she has been shot. The impression is that Mike is witnessing Susan's accident, even though they are separated by a long distance (and also chronologically). Again, this transition links acts of violence being committed by characters from developing countries, the apparent victims being members of the same U.S. family. Sometimes graphic matches substitute for continuity:

Chieko, crying, is cradled by detective Kenji in his arms, while Ahmed, who has just been shot by the police, is cradled by his distraught father. In this case, the situations of both teenagers are not easy to relate, yet we remain aware of the proximity between different types of trauma: Ahmed is dead, and his father can hardly comprehend what has happened; Chieko, affected by her mother's violent death, is undergoing pain that the young detective again cannot fathom. Yet both men respond in a physically similar fashion. Other transitions are less dramatic, or even comic: the laughter of two Japanese teenage girls is echoed by the bleating of goats in Morocco; or the same two girls standing inside Chieko's apartment are sutured together with the reflection in the water of the two Moroccan brothers, as if the ones were the flip side of the others. In transitions like these, it is less imperative to ascribe specific meanings to the cuts than to accept the pervasiveness and universality of a network society and a common humanity that make us all part of a common space (the contemporary space of flows) and a single story (that of people struggling, and often failing, to find solace and a scrap of happiness with others in the face of often fearful odds).

Formal connections between narrative blocks are not limited to visual strategies. The aural continuity between the girls and the goats is a relatively minor example of the sophisticated use of sound in *Babel*. In the following example, the connection carries much greater narrative weight: as Amelia is arrested by the immigration patrol and being taken into their truck, we hear Susan's voice asking Richard to take care of the children if she dies. Immediately, the image cuts to a shot of the Cate Blanchett character uttering the words. At this point, Amelia, the nurturing woman, is more worried about Mike and Debbie being lost in the desert than about her own future, so the sound bridge between the two stories contains several layers of irony, which reinforce the various contrasts between the two women, the undocumented immigrant's invisibility, and the mother's ignorance of important aspects of her children's identity, as well as their imminent danger. The visual contiguity between the two shots would have been sufficient to bring these meanings home, but the brief sound bridge welds the two women's feelings and priorities together, even though their situations are so far apart, and even though the events are not happening at the same time.

An earlier sound bridge is used more abstractly to suggest parallels and continuities between faraway spaces without specifying further: in one of the first changes of narrative blocks, the text moves from the night in the mountain village in the Moroccan mountains to the morning in the San Ysidro border crossing. The animated voice and music originating from Santiago's car radio in the latter location can already be briefly heard at the end of the shot of the inside of Ahmed and Yussef's hut. This transition highlights the contrast between the two places but more generally alerts the spectator to the workings of the multiprotagonist narrative and to the need to look for connections.

All the examples mentioned above are relatively rare cases of diegetic sound being used as part of a transition. In the final part of the movie, however, this function is carried by extradiegetic music. The first such transition is the graphic match of the two men cradling the dead Moroccan child and the ailing Japanese teenager in their arms, almost ninety minutes into the film. From that point on, most of the transitions are accompanied by external music that follows on from one block to the next. Twice in the film, the same melody connects not two but three narrative blocks, starting in the middle of one, continuing through the next one, and finishing in the third: in one case, the theme "Can I Be Forgiven?" starts when Susan is being carried into the helicopter to be evacuated from Tazarine, plays on in the scene with Chieko and Kenji, and is still heard for a few seconds at the beginning of the next scene, a detail shot of Amelia's nervous hands at the border-patrol station. At the end of this same narrative block, the last one of the Amelia story, the theme "Deportation" begins and then continues into the last scene of the Moroccan brothers' story. It then changes within this segment into the next melody, "Iguazu," which carries us into the next scene of Susan's evacuation from Tazarine by helicopter and arrival at the hospital in Casablanca. In the final forty minutes or so, therefore, extradiegetic music is permanently present at the transitions and openly changes the pattern established in the rest of the film.

This change contributes to an evolution in the general sense of the transitions. Although cuts between narrative blocks carry multiple meanings from the beginning and become the foundations of the filmic construction of an alternative space to the four geographical places of the stories, they tend to emphasize differences between these spaces and articulate the space of flows as a space of contrasts. This was the case, for example, with the false jump cut in the film's first transition: the similarities and visual continuity between the children's games call attention to the asymmetries and social imbalances between them. But now that music constantly spills from one block into the next, the distance between characters and spaces diminishes considerably. People throughout the world appear increasingly and irremediably intertwined, and the various extradiegetic tunes employed at these dense points of contact intensify the primacy of intense feelings in Iñárritu's space of flows.

Most of the original sound-track music in *Babel* was written and performed, as in Iñárritu's two earlier films, by Gustavo Santaolalla. For this one, Santaolalla decided to use the oud, an ancient Arabian string instrument, ancestor of the Spanish guitar, and perform all the melodies he composed for the film on it. Iñárritu has called this instrument the musical DNA of the picture, because it brings the three cultures together (García 259). This function is intensified in the final section of the film, where different melodies are not identified with specific stories but rather underline the parallels between them and their common emotional core. In the course of the narrative, the different musical themes suggest various moods and may evoke certain meanings, as happened with Chavela Vargas's song. However, their main role is to unify the four stories and narrative spaces through a series of variations that, in their diversity, are clearly recognizable as stemming from the same source, the unusual sound of the oud. In this sense, Santaolalla's music has a similar structure to the movie's color palette, with several variations around the basic idea of red, combined with different photographic styles for each of the stories (Bosley 1).

While the late meshing of spaces and narrative blocks through the proliferating musical bridges strengthens the common humanity toward which the film moves, the earlier scenes prepare the way for the final tour de force: from the beginning, the homogeneity of the musical themes alerts us to the need to understand the various stories together rather than in isolation. Without the metaphorical dimension of the transitions as representations of the border, the Santaolalla sound track carries an arguably stronger unifying function: the different melodies may suggest diverse emotions and feelings—anxiety, hope, melancholy, love, incomprehension, psychological and physical pain, intolerance, or desire—but they are all revealed to stem from the same root, the single note that according to Iñárritu floats above the four stories: the drive for intimacy (García 259). Whereas the transitions carry, like borders, the potential for separation or proximity, Santaolalla's music evokes a global world of easily translatable emotions that counteracts the dispersing effect of the biblical tower. It is significant in this sense that the last musical piece before the credits, "Bibo No Aozora," which is part of the *dénoument* of the Chieko story, was written and performed not by Santaolalla but by Ryuchi Sakamoto. Although the song is played with different instruments, the continuity with the rest of the music is remarkable, contributing to the last scene's special position in the narrative and to the general sense of interconnectedness between the different stories. While the various popular songs employed in *Babel,* whether diegetically or extradiegetically, may carry specific meanings, as in the case of "Tú me acostumbraste," the original sound track becomes the repository of a global space of feelings, an abstract but unmistakable force of emotional transnationality.

Music and editing, therefore, have a particularly crucial role in the construction of the film's space of flows and the articulation of the textual attitude toward borders. The transitions, as they have been interpreted here, are formal borders between the stories that enlarge the material signification of the concept to encompass broader senses. They call our attention to contrasts and dissimilarities between cultures, geopolitical circumstances, and feelings, but simultaneously, and gradually more intensely as the film develops, they visualize the potential of those cultures and feelings to come together in the space of the social and emotional borderlands. The structure of *Babel,* therefore, conveys the centrality of borders in all sorts of areas of contemporary experience while keeping a close focus on the materiality of one of the most densely traversed borders between nations in the world. Like the representation of the Tijuana–San Diego border, however, metaphorical borders are not restricted, in the film's narrative, to the moments of transition between blocks.

Several barriers fall in the film's various endings, borders between people becoming porous and fruitful places of exchange, but elsewhere in the film, the various spaces of places, to recuperate Castells's term for traditional forms of society, are equally traversed by borders. Shortly after arriving in Tazarine, with a bullet in her shoulder and in excruciating pain, Susan is left alone in a room with an old Berber woman, Anwar's grandmother (Sfia Ait Benboullah) (fig. 27). The Moroccan woman's radical otherness for the U.S. tourist is intensified by her extreme vulnerability in a life-and-death situation. At this point, the spectator may even recall Susan's admonition to her children that Mexico, the land where their nanny comes from, is a dangerous place. Alone in a remote desert village in Morocco, she comes face to face with her fears and intolerance toward the other. In the extremely poor dwelling, the border between the two women is almost visible, a thick line that separates apparently incommensurable identities.

Yet, as with the U.S.–Mexican border, the two women's attitudes are different depending on the side of the imaginary line. Sensing, from the silence of her apparently imposing otherness, Susan's vulnerability and anguish, the old woman immediately sets about creating a protective space for her ailing guest, sheltering her from the curious gaze of the children outside and stubbornly sitting next to her, in spite of Susan's initial guardedness, and giving her the basic comfort and warmth of physical proximity. In a matter of minutes, she has taken upon herself a parallel role to that of Amelia toward her children in the San Diego house. When, in the next block of this story, she lights her pipe and offers it to Susan, immediately managing to soothe her physical pain, the object becomes a symbol of the potential of the borderland to counteract the effect of

Figure 27. Soothing borderland: Susan meets Anwar's grandmother in *Babel*.

exclusionary boundaries and break barriers between people and a conduit of the type of exchange that can only happen in such charged places. Anwar's grandmother knows the protocol well, and, after the substance has made the desired effect, completely oblivious to the color of the skin and hair of the person who needs her help, she proceeds to caress her and speak to her in words that, beyond their superficial meaning, Susan can now perfectly understand. At this moment, the space between the two women having shrunk with unexpected intimacy, the space of the other has effortlessly become part of Susan's newborn identity.

The deployment of the border as both material geopolitical space and broader cultural concept allows Iñárritu to construct his stories around the pervasiveness of border experience in contemporary societies while at the same time vividly conveying the dangers, injustices, and discriminations involved in migrations, exiles, and diaspora. *Babel* concludes that, although some people are more immediately and traumatically affected by them than others, our world is increasingly defined by boundaries of all kinds. Accordingly, the film uses a panoply of formal devices and the conventions of the multiprotagonist genre to convey the central idea that, as García Canclini reminds us, today all cultures are border cultures (*Culturas* 316). While the various processes of economic and cultural globalization may have led some cultural critics to conclude that borders are becoming obsolete and national identities irrelevant (Appadurai 16; Naficy 124), Iñárritu's first three films show us that, on the contrary, they continue to occupy a central position in the definition of individual and group identities within a new transnational consciousness, in which, as Ezra and Rowden explain, nationalism remains "a canny dialogical partner" ("General" 4). The film, however, simultaneously shows that contemporary culture is moving beyond the restrictive framework of the nation-state (Shohat 53) and that new identities are being constructed around alternative spaces, which depend for their existence on nations and national identities but which in themselves transcend and deny the national. Deterritorialization has become not only a purely industrial concept, both in and outside the cinema, but a permanent condition of the transnational subject (Ezra and Rowden, "Introduction" 109) that inhabits simultaneously traditional spaces defined by physical places and virtual ones articulated through the network society. In *Babel,* the formal transitions between narrative blocks delineate subjects in a permanent state of transition, evoking Hamid Naficy's view that in a cinema defined by exile, diaspora, and migration, liminality and interstitiality are becoming important sources of creativity and dynamism (113). Through his sophisticated use of the generic conventions of the multiprotagonist film and his deployment of a multifaceted approach to modern time and space, Iñárritu has built a cinematic style and a very personal yet culturally relevant worldview around the interstices between shots, between places, between nations, and between narrative and chronological instants. Starting from a particular moment in the history of Mexican cinema, and from a particular place within Mexican culture, he has become the paragon of the contemporary filmmaker by appropriating and expanding the conventions of a new genre and constructing from the edges of the empire a new transnational citizenship and, in the process, a new object of cinematic fascination.

Interview with Alejandro González Iñárritu |

The following interview with Alejandro González Iñárritu took place in Barcelona on June 22, 2009, during a particularly busy period of postproduction for his film *Biutiful* and once we had finished writing our analysis of his work. In the course of the two-hour interview, the Mexican filmmaker answered our questions with generosity, kindness, depth, and intelligence, confirming in these and many other aspects that the unusual sophistication, compassion, and humanity that we have come to appreciate in his films are, at least in this case, an extension of the personality of their director. In the structure of the interview we tried to follow in part that of our critical commentary, but we finally let the proceedings be driven by Iñárritu's compelling and often mesmerizing discourse. The interview was conducted in Spanish and translated by the authors.

CELESTINO DELEYTO and MARÍA DEL MAR AZCONA: Do you like being described as a Mexican or a Latin-American filmmaker?

ALEJANDRO GONZÁLEZ IÑÁRRITU: It's a complex issue in the context of today's cinema because I think art should have no nationality. When a work of art is reduced to a geographical territory, often with a nationalistic sense, it's always diminished. This is a conflict or a misinterpretation that filmmakers like myself, who are always wandering from one place to another and making films all over, are often subject to. I am very proud of being Mexican, and I do believe that the point of view in my films is influenced by my nationality. As Baudelaire said, My childhood is my country. And it's true, my childhood and an important part of the rest of my life took place in Mexico, and this is something that will always impregnate my life and my work, everything I do and everything I say. If I had been born in the United States, my films would probably be very different. I want to have deep roots but lighter wings to fly, too. Nationalist cinema as a concept does not interest me. I don't believe in the labels of the New Mexican Cinema. There is one every three years. Which is the new one? Besides, when something is labeled as "new" it means that you will be the flavor of the month and then the next flavor will come soon. Those brands age very quickly.

CD and MA: What is your opinion of contemporary Hollywood cinema? Do you consider yourself part of it?

AGI: No, I do not consider myself part of Hollywood cinema, which is again too general a term. In the United States about seven hundred films are produced every year, and that's only the ones we hear about. Any film in English is immediately seen as a Hollywood film. It's a childish generalization, and there are prejudices even within the industry. The term "Hollywood movie" is often derogatory, so when somebody asks me whether mine are Hollywood films I never know whether they are praising them or insulting me. Some of the greatest films in history have been made within the Hollywood industry, and most of the great directors have worked there. But not all the films produced in the United States are Hollywood. There are scores, hundreds of independent companies that produce U.S. films in English and are not Hollywood even if they use actors from mainstream movies. That kind of combination exists. What do I think of Hollywood cinema? There's no simple answer: it has produced great films and bad films, it has the greatest directors, and it's a never-ending junk factory that too often follows trends, even fears. But that machine, which is always at work, all of a sudden produces a masterpiece because it has the structure, the skills. When somebody with the artistic inspiration arrives and impregnates the machine, the result is something wonderful.

I have never worked in Hollywood. My first film was totally independent, and so have been the other three. What do I mean by independent? I've developed my projects with total freedom and have financed them in different ways. I've conceived, written, or developed each of my scripts for a couple of years with no one around, and then I've financed the research, scouted the locations, and cast the films myself. Then I would present it to different possible backers saying, "This is the script, this is the cast, this is the cost. . . . Are you interested?" Not a word can be changed by contract, and I have had final cut since my first film. It's mine and only my responsibility. It's my philosophy that if I have to eat crap, at least it should be my own crap. I don't have any studio or anybody to blame. But even *Babel,* which at the core is a tough, deconstructed, foreign-language film with a high percentage of nonactors and new actors, gets distribution in the English-speaking territories by a company like Paramount and is then misjudged as a Hollywood film. For the Taliban independents, the fact of having Brad Pitt in one of the four stories seems to overshadow some of the risks and merits of the film in that area. This extreme way of judgment has become a ridiculous gimmick of the "intellectual police," as I call them.

My films have been financed through advanced international sales in different countries, and this diversification has helped me to keep even more control. But having access to the distribution machinery helps a film in the same way as a having a good editing house helps a book. You have more exposure to more people in the world without interfering with the content or the artist.

CD and MA: What do you think about the present situation of Mexican cinema? Do you still see yourself as an atypical director in the history of Mexican cinema?

AGI: Yes, I think I started off in the left lane and without a license. I was always an outsider. Nobody from that industry saw me coming. My first contact with Mexican cinema was when I was twenty. I was at the university studying cinema and media. A friend of mine had a production company that made very bad films, what we call in Mexico *ficheras* films, films about prostitutes. I wanted to be on a set. I asked my friend to ask his uncle, José Díaz, the company owner, to give me anything, a job carrying cables, whatever. And he sent me this message: "If you don't have relatives in Mexican cinema, go and find some." That was his literal answer. It was very tough, but that's how it worked. It was controlled by four or five families. The unions were also very difficult to get into. You had to belong to a family. So, I was always on the wrong side, and I had to do it my way and I'm grateful for that.

On the other hand, I admire the work of certain Mexican filmmakers who have survived brutal circumstances. Sometimes I may not even like their films, but I admire the perseverance, the stubbornness that is necessary to survive in such a situation. I identify with them in terms of cinematic militancy. But I think that the image projected by Mexican cinema is bipolar: if there's a new, interesting film, people immediately start again with the Mexican miracle. When you look at it, it's only one or two films every two years. The chain is as strong as its weakest link; it can break anywhere. There isn't a healthy Mexican industry, but there are the efforts of some extraordinary individual directors. Carlos Reygadas is an exceptional artist. I admire his films a great deal, and he has worked in extremely dire circumstances. He found his own way out in the context of a cinema with increasingly fewer spectators and less economic support. I also like the freshness of Fernando Eimbecke. These are two filmmakers from Mexico whose films I enjoy and who have interesting things to say. Their commitment and their artistry are extraordinary, but they don't belong to or are not a consequence of a strong Mexican industry. They are the result of their own individual talent.

CD and MA: Do you think there is a link between the violence and suffering that can be seen in *Amores perros* and your country's cultural identity?

AGI: Maybe but there's as much suffering in Mexico as in any European or Asian country. I don't think we're different from anywhere else in that sense. I prefer to explore suffering from the perspective of the circumstances that lead characters to extreme situations. Those events cause pain, and pain is inevitable in our lives. Suffering is optional, but pain is inevitable. You can't understand or speak in any depth about life except from the perspective of death. I mean, you can't enjoy life fully ignoring or rejecting that some day it will end. We live in a pasteurized society, which sells the idea that you have to avoid pain, that pain shouldn't exist, but that's an illusion. They sell us products and holidays all to make us ephemerally happy. The United States as a society doesn't accept the reality of suffering. They live in the constant illusion that you mustn't age, you must always be happy. It's all appearance. They evade pain—they do not exude it; they do not talk about it. Most of the films don't represent anything that's really human. There's always escapism in the fashion in which those issues are handled. This is why many people, especially in the United States, are shocked by my films and tell me, "There's too much pain in your movies." But you suffer when your child dies, or when you make a mistake, or make the wrong decision. I like to explore human beings coping with their suffering, confronting it, and recovering from it. In my films I've always tried to find redemption, some sort of evolution in a different direction, the attainment of a certain purity, coming out on the other side with a luminosity that wasn't there before. That's what I like about suffering. I don't think it's enough to put people inside a tunnel, close the door, and turn the lights off. My films travel through very dark moments, but I try to see the light at the end. I think life is like that. We all have transitional moments—at work, in a relationship. It's like the yin and the yang. I'm not saying anything new.

The same can be said about violence. Unjustified explicit violence bothers me a lot. The culture of shock has always been a refuge for those who have nothing to say, and today it's very profitable. So, just as bad architects usually make very big buildings, nowadays to shock is a great temptation for someone who has nothing to say. And by the way, it's very easy to do it.

What bothers me is the uncultured, childish, frivolous, stupid attitude of directors old enough to know better who take advantage of the video-game generation, the victims of the marketing machinery of this cynical industry. They make films in the nonstory/pure-action-dude mold. Films! The Manicheanism and the archetypes are needed when you are a kid, but to keep feeding people with those black-and-white, noncomplex endings and stories is unbelievable. I think violence in my films always has brutal consequences. I never trivialize violence because I am from a violent country, and I know what it is to live in fear and experience it and to suffer its consequences. The chopped-off heads that appear in my country every day are unfortunately not from a video game, and neither is the suffering of the kids in the war that these stupid video games ignore or avoid. I try to explore human behavior through a violent event or a violent act with a fatal outcome. Death has weight in my films. It's important. When a character dies, it's not like a pebble falling on the ground. It makes a difference. I think nowadays people run away from those realities.

CD and MA: What do borders mean to you?

AGI: Borders were invented by human beings. When I go to the seaside, what I find hypnotic about the sea, what is truly relaxing, is that there's no property. If an idiot decided to build a brick wall in the sea, if the technical possibility existed, I'm sure all the G-8 countries would erect a barrier in the sea. Borders are ideological and nationalistic territories that make us smaller. It's the same with artistic borders. The most dangerous borders are the ideological, not the physical ones. That's a very serious problem. Those are the borders that really scare me. Also spiritual and religious borders. They're very hard to get rid of.

CD and MA: Has your attitude toward material borders changed since you've lived in Los Angeles?

AGI: It's a terrible, abusive border. It's the border of a country with an intolerable double moral standard. A country that talks about freedom in the world and sells weapons to defend freedom, and yet they have the biggest wall ever built against a neighbor country. We are not terrorists; we are not dangerous. They criticize others for precisely what they do in their own back yard. They're proud to have brought about the demolition of the Berlin Wall, and they have their own in the south. It's a brutal reality. I cross the border every six months to renew my visa, and when you go down from San Diego there's nobody to stop you. We Mexicans have such low self-esteem; we are so oppressed. I once asked the ambassador, "Why don't you at least set up a border booth?" You can drive through in your car, you can have people kidnapped in your trunk or an atomic bomb. Nobody will stop you. Americans can come into our country anytime they like because they're American. We can get the worst trash in the whole universe, and we have no control over what went through. On the other hand, when you return it's neverending queues and a ritual of humiliation. It's very unfair. It's a very unbalanced border.

CD and MA: What can you tell us about your personal experience and that of your family as foreigners in the United States?

AGI: On a personal level, I must say that I've had a very privileged experience. Alfonso Cuarón once said that we are *braceros de lujo* [wetbacks deluxe]. I laughed, but I think he was right. I have a very critical view of that double moral standard that Americans have been playing with and of the way they've been taking advantage of Mexican labor in both countries. Both Mexico and the United States have profited from illegal immigrants who have no rights, work hours on end, and are the second source of income for my country. Without them, Mexico would collapse economically. They sustain whole areas of the U.S. economy precisely because both countries have not negotiated an agreement, because it's not in their interest. They're always complaining about each other but do nothing to solve the problem. Yet, on a personal level, my experience has been extraordinary. Why? Because I'm a person with a certain intellectual level. I'm a professional. My case is not at all representative of the experience of Mexicans in the United States. I've always felt welcome and received support. And we all know that it's an extraordinary society in many ways. There's a very modern, progressive, artistic side, and a wonderful community with great people. We go back to the issue of labels. In my country I've been accused of going over to the gringos, but the gringos are a very complex multiethnic society with more than 350 million people that live in one of the most interesting societies in the world, at least from an artistic point of view. On the other hand, they have a cruel, primitive side. Personally, I've been on the side I like, and I have learned to be happy there. Mexicans have a sort of natural relationship with the United States. It's always been there as a border, but also as an aspiration. Our proximity to the United States and its cultural products causes an intrinsic desire to have access to other cultures, and that gives us a cultural advantage. Who wouldn't recognize that great literature, films, music, painting, and even Internet have been generated there? Even the fact of having a black president has put them again years ahead of Europe, for example. The United States has always been very interesting in that respect.

When I arrived in Los Angeles, it was four days before 9/11. Then, all of a sudden, everything changed. Fear took over, and there started to grow a new racism based on fear. Fortunately, although my family arrived in the country in that context, my children never had any problems of adaptation. We found a very interesting school for our children. Its motto is to celebrate difference. Americans love the word "tolerance." I hate that word. We shouldn't just tolerate difference; we must *celebrate* it. That school tries to celebrate the multiethnic side of the city by keeping the exact proportion of multiethnicity in its premises that will reflect the ethnic makeup of Los Angeles. It was that particular school that made us decide to stay. We would have never found that type of school in Mexico. It's also a socially minded school. It has children from all social strata, and that makes for a very real experience for my children.

Los Angeles is a very complex, contradictory city. It's a kind of human experiment in an ideal geographical environment, but it also has serious social deficiencies. There's a feeling of loneliness, but it's a loneliness that everybody accepts and lives with, because there's also this need to succeed. The reasons why people arrive there are relatively similar. Everybody shares this dream, and the result is a community of the desolate. There's a kind of nostalgia for the success you'll never have. People stay there, floating, because returning would be admitting failure. As Baudrillard said, it's the first primitive society of the future. I love that definition. It's the only society where people haven't lost the capacity to dream. They create a lot of rubbish, but all of a sudden somebody arrives one day with a great idea, and nobody could have made it anywhere else in the world. They get enthusiastic about impossible ideas. In France, for example, they're unfazed about new ideas: they say they've seen everything. They've lost the capacity for enthusiasm. Los Angeles is an enthusiastic, adolescent city. I think of it as a sixteen-year-old girl.

CD and MA: Could you tell us why all your films so far have been multiprotagonist films? Was it a premeditated decision, or did it just happen?

AGI: There's not just one single reason. I've thought about it, and I guess it's a consequence of several things that happened at particular moments. On the one hand, that's basically the way my father tells stories, and that was a primary influence. He's a fantastic storyteller, and it always struck me that he told stories in a scrambled manner. He started at the end, then went to the beginning, and then to the middle. He was telling a story about somebody who'd just been sent to jail, and then he started telling you about this person's great-grandfather. And then you said to him, "But what happened to him in jail?" And he replied, "Wait and see, let me tell you about his great-grandfather." And then you realized that the great-grandfather's episode was crucial to understand something that had happened to this person in jail. My father has a natural-born talent to know when to reveal information when telling a story, and that's mainly what storytelling is about.

On the other hand, scrambled narratives are quite common in Latin American literature: Julio Cortázar, Jorge Luis Borges, Ernesto Sábato—they are all writers I was really impressed with when I first read them. I guess that navigating between parallel stories is something very common in Latin American literature. There were also cinematic influences. I was really impressed by *Rashomon* when I saw it as a student. Then there were also *Before the Rain* and *Smoke,* which is not actually multiprotagonist but has a multiprotagonist touch in its proliferation of stories.

Also, before I made *Amores perros,* I had also directed lots of commercials. I was probably the director that spent the most time on a movie set. I lived on the set 180 days a year. I was there writing, filming, and editing the commercials, and all that work gave me a lot of filmic skills. But I really wanted to do something that lasted longer than one minute. Then there came the possibility of getting some funding from IMCINE [Instituto Mexicano de Cinematografía] to shoot several short films. I thought about directing a multiprotagonist experiment, which consisted of ten shorts of one minute each that took place in the same city and were structured around a central event: a fire. There was one story of a couple who was having an argument, and then the girl turned around and saw smoke coming from a stadium. There was another story about a group of boys who were going to the stadium and lost their tickets. The fire could never be seen directly. You could see it in the eyes of a group of young children who were looking at it, but never directly. It was a very ambitious project. It was at that moment that I met Guillermo Arriaga, and we started to write this multiprotagonist exercise. It was fun creating a whole narrative out of different snatches of life taking place simultaneously. The funding never came through, and Guillermo and I decided to write a movie. We had several stories we wanted to tell, and we started to meet quite regularly to write a script. That was the origin of *Amores perros*. It wasn't a premeditated decision. It came quite naturally as a consequence of that idea of ten shorts that was never made.

CD and MA: And what about the other two?

AGI: Guillermo told me one day that he had an idea about a man who was dying and needed a heart transplant. He was fascinated by it but needed a way to develop it and some additional contextual elements. I suggested that he write a storyline, and then we'd start from there. He wrote twenty pages of a story that was completely linear. I read it and saw that something wasn't working there. Everything seemed quite predictable. I immediately realized that the story would benefit from a scrambled narrative structure, because that way predictability would become inevitability. And inevitability, as opposed to predictability, can be very interesting when telling a story. *21 Grams* had a potential radioactive problem: it deals with pure melodramatic elements that can be found one way or another in the soap-opera world. I knew I was dealing with something that needed a radically different approach and execution. The structure was crucial to it, not to mention the register and the performances, which were delightful. Yet, in this type of experiment with narrative structure, there's always a potential problem. When a scrambled narrative structure is not at the service of the story, it becomes just an ornament, and it limits rather than enhances the content. Unfortunately, those empty narrative games are quite common nowadays.

Regarding the structure, *21 Grams* was by far the most complex of the three movies. I wanted each scene to be completely unrelated to the previous and the following ones. Initially, there was also a juxtaposition of night and day scenes that I also tried to use in *Babel,* until it started to affect the story and became a constraint. In the case of *21 Grams,* the form is essential to the content and the themes of the film. It's a powerful and excruciating story, and the structure is crucial. Yet, the risk was always there. I was afraid that spectators would see the movie as a puzzle to be solved. I didn't want them to think too much about the structure. I was looking for an emotional structure in a completely atemporal storyline. This is one of the risks of this type of structures. You don't want to lose your audience emotionally, which is very difficult. *21 Grams* is probably the movie that I've rewritten most times in the editing room. I was looking for the right way for things to work emotionally. So in the case of *21 Grams*, it was a conscious and deliberate way of making the story stronger. It was very risky, but I think it worked in the end. I always saw it as an extreme experiment with narrative structure.

After *21 Grams, Babel* was an almost logical evolution to put an end to my filmic experiments with scrambled multiprotagonist structures. At the beginning there were five stories that we had to reduce to four because otherwise the movie would have been too long. This time the structure was clear from the very beginning. *Babel* is the culmination of my exploration of scrambled narrative patterns. It's a fragmented emotional experience, which is, after all, what cinema is about. Movies rely on the juxtaposition of several elements that, from a rational point of view, shouldn't provoke any kind of emotional reaction, but our brain links these two images, and there's an emotion. And that's the experiment of these three films. As long as the emotional pulse is still there, the experiment is a beautiful one.

CD and MA: So *Biutiful* is not a multiprotagonist film?

AGI: When *Babel* premiered at Cannes, I already said that it was my last experiment with this type of narrative structures. After linking stories taking place in three continents in *Babel*, I don't think I can expand the pattern any more. I really enjoyed experimenting with narrative structures in the three films. I was aware that I was taking lots of risks, and I found that very exciting. But after *Babel* I also started to feel that I was being typecast. I didn't want people to go to see my next movie thinking, "Let's see Alejandro González Iñárritu's new temporal game." Then that movie wasn't going to be inevitable, as was the case with *Babel*, but predictable. If I'm just the scrambled storyteller, then I'll just be like one of those artists who paints a masterpiece and that's it. I also realized that there was a proliferation of movies using this type of narrative structure.

I know that the structure is as old as the cinema. I didn't invent it. But suddenly it became more and more popular. It was used once and again, and I thought it became slightly overused. You need to move on. I like what I did in *Amores perros, 21 Grams,* and *Babel,* and if somebody likes the pattern and wants to use it, that's okay, but I don't want to do that anymore. I need to move on and do something different. I met Ferrán Adriá [the famous Spanish chef], and I asked him, "You have forty-two people working in your kitchen. How do you know that these people aren't going to take your recipes and open restaurants all over the world?" And he said, "I don't care. I close my restaurant for six months a year. I think about my new recipes for the next year, and when I open again the following year it's never the same menu. They can copy my recipes and open their own restaurants because I know I won't be doing them anymore." I really liked his answer. You can't just do the same thing once and again. You need to move on.

CD and MA: How important is music in your films? And sound in general?

AGI: Sound is 50 percent of a movie and sometimes even more. I have a better ear than I have an eye. In a way, I'm a frustrated musician. When I make a movie, I'm very interested in the transitions, and not only in the visual ones. When I'm working on the script, I'm already thinking about how I'll cut from one scene to the next. I'm very interested in the transitions between different geographical locations. The spectator has to move seamlessly in the transitions from one scene to another. And the sound is a crucial part of that. Every single sound that takes place in the transitions of my movies is absolutely deliberate. Martín Hernández is in charge of that. He has been working with me for almost thirty years. And with Gustavo Santaolalla, I've found the kind of minimalist music that I needed. I'm not interested in music that emphasizes what you can already see. I like it when the music adds something new or different to what's being shown. I don't like to have a lot of music in my movies. I only use it when it's absolutely necessary or when I think that it will add something.

CD and MA: Why does handheld camera predominate in your films?

AGI: Handheld camera is very often accused of being an artificial element, but I always defend its potential when used in the right way. I think that the handheld camera is the closest you can get to the way the human being experiences the world. We see through a handheld camera. When I move around, I don't dolly or crane. Like the tripod, those are antinatural ways of experiencing the world. The handheld camera is the way to see the world as the character is experiencing it. I'm not against those other techniques, but the handheld camera seems more natural to me. When I design a scene with Rodrigo Prieto, with whom I've been working for more than eighteen years, I tell him what part of each shot I'm interested in. We talk about the scene, we place the actors in the scene, and then we subordinate the camera to all those elements. The camera is there to enhance what I want to show at that specific moment. From the angle to the type of lens, everything is subordinated to the content of the scene and the feeling I want to convey. We talk about that until the camera becomes a narrative tool capable of creating different feelings, like uncertainty or peace. It points at what I, as a spectator, should half see—it suggests, it narrates. We've also used it in *Biutiful.* In this film, it's a special handheld camera because we use it according to the needs of the character. It creates different sensations depending on the moment. This is something that I couldn't have done in any of my other films. It becomes organic. Some people accuse the handheld camera of being manipulative. They say, leave the frame and allow the spectators to see what they want to see. This is what Jim Jarmusch does. I like the way he uses the camera, but not for my films. There's no free will in my case. I want to tell the story the way I want to tell it.

CD and MA: What's the role of fate and chance in the life of human beings?

AGI: I think both are very important. We need to believe that we own our destiny, that we build it. Yet we all know that there are events and circumstances that take place, usually against our will and wishes, that have absolutely nothing to do with us. A very important part of what we are is how we react to those events. We react to a crisis, to an illness, to a tragic event. We also generate things ourselves, but to a much lesser extent. These events force us to make decisions and confront us with our deepest feelings and our links with other human beings. That's one of the things I tried to explore in these three films. How does somebody react to an accidental and tragic event? Where's the line between destiny and coincidence? It's difficult to tell. But I personally think that it is our reactions to things that move the world. There is this sentence that my father used to say and that has always traumatized me. I used it in *Amores perros:* "If you want to make God laugh, tell him your plans." I think this sentence impregnates the three films. It could even be the closing line of the trilogy.

CD and MA: You have said that with *Amores perros,* you wanted to represent through love the suffering and complexity of a city like Mexico

City. Do you think that the multiprotagonist structure of your films has something to do with your own experience as a citizen of Mexico City?

AGI: I've always seen Mexico City as an anthropological experiment. It's a very dynamic and complex city. I didn't want to show the city. I didn't want to show any of the icons of the city. The film is very Mexican, but you can't see Mexico in it. It's not a movie about the city as an architectural space but about its people. I think it catches some of the energy of Mexico City. I wouldn't call it a Mexican but a *chilango* film. It's about the city. Somebody who has lived in Mexico City knows that that's where the heart of Mexico beats, with its good and its bad things.

CD and MA: Both in *Amores perros* and *Babel* there's a clear intention to identify the names of the locations where the action is taking place. Why is the filmic city in *21 Grams* never specified?

AGI: Originally the story of *21 Grams* took place in Mexico. But then I started to become very interested in the element of guilt in the Benicio del Toro character, which wasn't in the script at the very beginning. And I thought that the element of guilt would be better portrayed in the United States, especially in the South, where religious communities like the one that appears in the film abound. I was looking for certain textures. On the other hand, I didn't want to locate the film in Los Angeles or New York. I find Los Angeles a pasteurized city. I traveled a lot around the United States, scouting locations. In Memphis I found a touch of decadence and sadness. It retains a certain flavor. I liked the way it looked in the fall, when we went to shoot there. I like the grey palette of the city. I don't like to use the color green in my movies. I don't like green pastures or trees. I wanted the feeling of a grey city, one that spectators wouldn't immediately identify. Then there was the question of accents. The actors asked me if they had to speak like people in Memphis. I said no, because I didn't really care how people from Memphis speak. The film was not about that. It wasn't a documentary. So it was a creative decision, but I shot the film in Memphis because of the textures and the pervading sense of melancholy that inundates the city.

CD and MA: What can you tell us about the empty pool at the motel in *21 Grams*?

AGI: Empty pools are one of my most recurrent nightmares. There's also an empty pool in *Amores perros*. The dog-fighting arena is actually an empty pool. They reflect decadence and abandon, the sense of something that's already gone. To me, an empty pool represents many things: lack of presence, lack of care, something that was and is no longer there. It's an image with a great emotional charge, like dry leaves. I liked the motel, and I loved that empty pool. It's a sterile space, like a dry womb. The snow in 21 Grams was completely unplanned, but it became one of my favorite moments. We were filming, and it started to snow, and I told everybody to get their cameras and start shooting. I wasn't sure whether I was going to use it, but I thought it was a beautiful image and a gift from Nature. After all the neglect and the decay, everything starts to get clean again. There's light at the end of the tunnel.

CD and MA: The last shot of Babel is impressive because of its beauty and the amount of meanings it suggests. Could you tell us a little bit about what you were trying to get across in it?

AGI: That's an example of the type of shot I call el abandonador: a shot in which we go from being very close to the characters, almost able to smell their skin, to giving them some space to breathe and look at them from a distance. The one in Babel required a lot of work. I thought of it almost at the end of the shooting, and everybody in the crew got mad at me. It required a completely different cinematographic language, but I thought it was essential to show the loneliness and the nakedness of characters in a city of millions of people. It's like pulling back from the beehive to see that what we've just seen is only one of the myriad stories taking place in the city. I told you just one, but there are millions like this.

CD and MA: What's your opinion of Amelia's return to Tijuana after all those years in the United States? Do you consider it a personal defeat, or is there hope in this return?

AGI: I think there's hope. She has just suffered the extreme humiliation of being deported, but I wanted to have her son go and meet her at the border. That wasn't in the original script, in which Amelia ended the film alone, sitting on the curb. But I can't do that to my characters because I love them too much, and that's why I had her son go to meet her. So that final scene is saying, well, you lost your job, you lost the United States, but you won your family. You're welcome in your country, and you're hugged by your son who loves you. We've seen the way her family lives in Mexico, and we can imagine how much she misses all that. The character of Amelia is loosely based on Julia, a Mexican woman that works for my family. She comes from Oaxaca, and she's always telling us fascinating stories about her life there. She shows us videos, and we can perceive her nostalgia. Yet, she doesn't want to go back to Mexico. It looks fun from the distance, but she is very much aware of the difficulties of life there. The men are very sexist. Her own husband abandoned her. So she prefers to live in the States, half-numb but away from it all. Yet you can see that she misses it a lot. It's a very complex experience.

CD and MA: Some critics have referred to your movies as "the trilogy of suffering." Would you agree with that? Do you consider your films pessimistic?

AGI: No, I don't. I think they are realistic. What I've always tried to do is make people think and reflect about a specific issue. I don't like closed endings. I've always tried to leave an open door, and it's very much up to the experience of each individual spectator where the characters are going to go after that. I've also talked to people who think that the endings of my movies are always hopeful. When you see el Chivo walking away at the end of *Amores perros,* his walk toward an uncertain future feels like a form of regeneration. He rises like a phoenix from the ashes. He is somebody who's going to start anew, who's just got rid of his shell of dirt and walks away clean and shaven. He is going to fly now. He is moved and has repented from his past decisions. He's been given the chance to be reborn. Likewise with Cristina in *21 Grams:* she finds herself pregnant again, with the opportunity to reinvent herself and start a new life. In *Babel,* father and daughter hold hands and embrace each other. So do Richard and Susan, and in Morocco the father embraces his dead son. Amelia's son is also waiting for her in Tijuana to embrace her.

Then there's the case of Octavio in *Amores perros.* I like his final moment. He's a fool, a silly teenager, a bastard, but that moment when Susana doesn't come to the station is crucial for him. He is clean-shaven, and he is hurting, but life has taught him a lesson. He'll never be so stubborn again. Some friends said that he should have got on the bus, but that would have been wrong. It would have meant that he hadn't learned anything. He must realize that he messed up, that he hurt other people. He's a teenager who's learned his lesson the hard way. People go through extreme pain, but that experience serves them to reinvent themselves, or to rediscover themselves or the other. I always try to point out that possibility. I don't know whether that's optimism or not, but for me it's realism, it's human truth. Pain is inevitable. I try to capture it, photograph it, x-ray it, but I never poke into it or describe it as the only way. Pain teaches us very profound things about human nature.

CD and MA: Several critics have pointed out that you never pass judgment on your characters. Do you think your films have a moral sense? What kind of values do they defend? What's their moral structure?

AGI: I guess all my movies are very similar to one another in that way because they are very personal films. Every movie is impregnated, whether you like it or not, by the personality of its director. I've met many directors all over the world, and it's always struck me how a movie resembles its director. It's incredible. A movie is something so personal that you can't escape from it. It's like drawing: the colors and the format you choose, they all say a lot about you. You just couldn't say that's not you. I love my characters, and a common feature to most of them is their ambivalence. There's a lot of compassion in them. That could be a common feature to them all. They could be horrible people, but they are not. I remember being worried about el Chivo. He is a hired assassin; he tortures people. Yet my aim was to make him believable and lovable. He's a killer, but he moves us, and we can understand him. I'm always looking for the human being behind the actor. And I really hope that that compassion that I am always looking for shines through in my films. They're complex characters.

What the main character in *Biutiful* does for a living is quite questionable. I showed the movie to somebody the other day, and he said to me that he didn't really understand the character. So I asked him, "What don't you understand about him?" And he said, "I don't know whether he is good or bad." To me that's the best compliment, because it's precisely what I'm looking for. I try to create three-dimensional characters. We're all like that. We are many things at the same time, and it's impossible to categorize people as just good or bad.

CD and MA: You've already said that *Biutiful* is not a multiprotagonist film. Are there any other differences between this movie and the previous ones?

AGI: The structure of *Biutiful* is strictly and rigorously linear. I really wanted to do something new, which was to get immersed in the journey of one single character from his point of view. I found the experience fascinating, even if for others it may be quite normal. Some people may think that multiprotagonist structures are more complex than single-hero ones, but they're also simpler in that the stories are shorter: each story is no more than twenty-eight or thirty pages. They are different narrative exercises.

I don't think that I could have made this movie a couple of years ago because it requires a very precise knowledge of how narratives work, and I wasn't used to that. Sometimes in a multiprotagonist film, if there's a crack in one of the narrative arcs, you can just cut to another storyline, and you can distract the audience. That's not the case in a movie like *Biutiful.* The slightest chink makes the whole narrative structure crumble and collapse. I found out that my old ways of dealing with and revealing information didn't work here. Another important difference is that while my three previous films are plot-driven, *Biutiful* is character-driven. In *Amores perros, 21 Grams,* and *Babel,* there's an event that happens very early in the narrative that makes the plot move forward. I already knew where to put all the narrative hooks. In *Biutiful,* the narrative pace is completely different. The first small event takes place around page thirty or thirty-five of the script. It requires completely different skills. It was very traumatic at the beginning, but now I think the whole experience was beautiful. It works through the accumulation of very little, almost insignificant events that in the end gather a powerful force. It's a little gust that ends as a tsunami. Unlike the tumult of the previous ones, the ostensible noise, this film was fascinating because it was like dampness: it wets you gradually, almost imperceptibly, and when you realize it you are soaking wet and asking yourself, "When did I get drenched?" The result is deafening, as in the other films, but in this case it is the sum total of a number of things. It was a very difficult film to make, but also very beautiful and exciting.

That's the structural difference with the others. And there's also the experience of working with only one protagonist. You have to enter a universe with only one other person. I was used to working with actors for three weeks, then another set of actors for another three weeks, and so on. The change in that respect was also particularly demanding. It requires a different kind of discipline and a new language. It was much more intense. I underestimated what it would require, and it turned out to be much more complex than *Babel.* It was a wonderful experience, and I'm very excited. It was a new challenge to tell only one story. The others were fragmented experiences, and this one was monolithic. I was with some musician friends of mine yesterday, and I was telling them that I had always seen *Amores perros* as rock, *21 Grams* as jazz, and *Babel* as a piece of eclectic music. *Biutiful* is like the blues: a long, melancholy note.

/

Amores perros (Love's a bitch; 2000)
Mexico
Production: Zeta Film, AltaVista Films
Producer: Alejandro González Iñárritu
Associate Producers: Raúl Olvera Ferrer, Guillermo Arriaga, Pelayo
  Gutiérrez, Mónica Lozano Serrano
Executive Producers: Martha Sosa Elizondo, Francisco González Compeán
Screenplay: Guillermo Arriaga
Director of Photography: Rodrigo Prieto
Editors: Alejandro González Iñárritu, Luis Carballar, Fernando Pérez Unda
Music: Gustavo Santaolalla
Art Director: Melo Hinojosa
Set Decorator: Julieta Álvarez
Production Designer: Brigitte Broch
Costume Designer: Gabriela Diaque
Make-up Artists: David Gameros, Marco Rosado
Sound: Antonio Diego
Sound Designer: Martín Hernández
Sound Editors: Joaquín Díaz, Efraín García Mora, Alejandro Quevedo,
  Rodolfo Romero, Adrián Reynoso
Cast: Emilio Echevarría (El Chivo), Gael García Bernal (Octavio), Goya
  Toledo (Valeria), Álvaro Guerrero (Daniel), Vanessa Bauche (Susana),
  Jorge Salinas (Luis), Marco Pérez (Ramiro), Rodrigo Murray (Gustavo),
  Humberto Busto (Jorge), Gerardo Campbell (Mauricio), Adriana Barraza
  (Octavio's mother), José Sefami (Leonardo), Lourdes Echevarría (Maru),
  Laura Almela (Julieta), Ricardo Dalmacci (Andrés Salgado), Gustavo
  Sánchez Parra (Jarocho)
Color
154 min.

11'09"01—September 11 (2002)
France
Production: Galatée Films, Studio Canal
Executive Producer: Jean de Trégomain
Line Producers: Jacques Perrin, Nicolas Mauvernay
Original Idea: Alain Brigand
Mexico Segment:
Production: Zeta Films, Anonymous Content
Producers: Alejandro González Iñárritu, Gustavo Santaolalla
Associate Producer: Emilio Azcárraga
Executive Producers: Pelayo Gutiérrez, Shelly Townsend
Screenplay: Alejandro González Iñárritu
Editors: Alejandro González Iñárritu, Robert Duffy, Kim Bica
Sound Designers: Martín Hernández, Alejandro González Iñárritu
Music: Gustavo Santaolalla, Osvaldo Golijov
Associate Music Producer: Anibal Kerpel
Postproduction Supervisor: David Glean
Special Effects: Kathy Siegel, Mandy L. Tankenson, Mark Franco, Andy
    Rafael Barrios
Color
11 min.
Additional segments by Samira Makhmalbaf ("God, Construction, and
    Destruction"), Claude Lelouch ("France"), Youssef Chahine ("Egypt"),
    Danis Tanovic ("Bosnia-Herzegovina"), Idrissa Ouédraogo ("Burkina
    Faso"), Ken Loach ("United Kingdom"), Amos Gitai ("Israel"), Mira Nair
    ("India"), Sean Penn ("USA"), Shohei Imamura ("Japan")

21 Grams (2003)
USA, Germany
Production: This Is That, Y Productions, Mediana Productions
Producers: Alejandro González Iñárritu, Robert Salerno
Associate Producer: Guillermo Arriaga
Executive Producer: Ted Hope
Screenplay: Guillermo Arriaga
Director of Photography: Rodrigo Prieto
Editor: Stephen Mirrione
Music: Gustavo Santaolalla
Art Director: Deborah Riley
Set Designer: Thomas Betts
Set Decorator: Meg Everist
Production Designer: Brigitte Broch
Costume Designer: Marlene Stewart

Make-up Artist: Luisa Abel
Sound Designers: Martín Hernández, Roland Thai
Sound Editors: Sergio Díaz, Michael Hertlein, Michael Mullane, Robert
    Getty
Cast: Sean Penn (Paul Rivers), Naomi Watts (Cristina Peck), Danny Huston
    (Michael), Carly Nahon (Katie), Claire Pakis (Laura), Benicio Del Toro
    (Jack Jordan), Charlotte Gainsbourg (Mary Rivers), Eddie Marsan
    (Reverend John), Melissa Leo (Marianne Jordan), Marc Thomas Musso
    (Freddy), Teresa Delgado (Gina), Clea DuVall (Claudia), Jerry Chipman
    (Cristina's Father)
Color
124 min.

Babel (2006)
USA, Mexico, France
Production: Anonymous Content, Zeta Film, Central Films
Producers: Alejandro González Iñárritu, Jon Kilik, Steve Golin
Coproducer: Ann Ruark
Associate Producer: Corinne Golden Weber
Screenplay: Guillermo Arriaga
Director of Photography: Rodrigo Prieto
Editors: Stephen Mirrione, Douglas Crise
Music: Gustavo Santaolalla
Art Directors: Claudia Vásquez Lostau (Mexico), Rio Sujimoto (Japan)
Production Designer: Brigitte Broch
Set Decorators: Mohamed Rekka (Morocco Crew), Yoshihito Akatsuka
    (Japan)
Costume Designers: Michael Wilkinson, Gabriela Diaque, Miwako Kobayashi
Make-up Artists: Alessandro Bertolazzi (Key Make-up Artist, Morocco
    Crew), Mutsuki Sakai (Key Make-up Artist, Japan), Alfredo Mora (Chief
    Make-up Artist, Mexico)
Sound Designer: Martín Hernández
Cast: Brad Pitt (Richard Jones), Cate Blanchett (Susan), Mohamed Akhzam
    (Anwar), Sfia Ait Benboullah (Anwar's Grandmother), Boubker Ait El
    Caid (Yussef), Said Tarchani (Ahmed), Mustapha Rachidi (Abdullah),
    Abdelkader Bara (Hassan), Adriana Barraza (Amelia), Elle Fanning
    (Debbie Jones), Nathan Gamble (Mike Jones), Gael García Bernal
    (Santiago), Robert 'Bernie' Esquivel (Luis), Rinko Kikuchi (Chieko
    Wataya), Kôji Yakusho (Yasujiro Wataya), Satoshi Nikaido (Det. Lt. Kenji
    Mamiya)
Color
143 min.

Biutiful (2010)
Spain, Mexico
Production: Cha Cha Cha, Focus Features, Mod Producciones, Universal
  Pictures
Producers: Fernando Bovaira, Alfonso Cuarón, Alejandro González Iñárritu,
  Guillermo del Toro
Screenplay: Alejandro González Iñárritu, Armando Bo, Nicolás Giacobone
Director of Photography: Rodrigo Prieto
Editor: Stephen Mirrione
Music: Gustavo Santaolalla
Art Director: Marina Pozanco
Production Designer: Brigitte Broch
Costume Designer: Sabine Daigeler, Paco Delgado
Make-up Artist: Alessandro Bertolazzi
Sound: José Antonio García
Sound Designer: Martín Hernández
Cast: Javier Bardem (Uxbal), Blanca Portillo, Rubén Ochandiano, Eduard
  Fernández, Ana Wagener, Maricel Álvarez, Jesús Puchol, Diana Aymerich
Color

References

Acevedo-Muñoz, Ernesto R. "Sex, Class, and Mexico in Alfonso Cuarón's *Y tu mamá también.*" *Film and History* 34.1 (2004): 39–48.

Anzaldúa, Gloria. *Borderlands/La Frontera: The New Mestiza.* 2d ed. San Francisco: Aunt Lute Books, 1999.

Appadurai, Arjun. *Modernity at Large: Cultural Dimensions of Globalization.* Minneapolis: University of Minnesota Press, 1996.

Arriaga, Guillermo. "Introduction: Structure and Character in *Amores Perros.*" In *Amores Perros* (Original Screenplay). Trans. Alan Page. London: Faber and Faber, 2001. vii–xi.

———. "Life Goes On" (Interview with Kevin Conroy Scott). In *21 Grams* (Original Screenplay). Trans. Alan Page. London: Faber and Faber, 2003. ix–xxiii.

Audeé, Françoise. "*Amours chiennes*: Désirs aveugles, fantômes futurs." *Positif* 477 (November 2000): 22–23.

Ayala Blanco, Jorge. *La fugacidad del cine mejicano.* Mexico City: Océano, 2001.

Babel. Press kit. Paramount Pictures, 2006.

Baer, Hester, and Ryan Long. "Transnational Cinema and the Mexican State in Alfonso Cuarón's *Y tu mamá también.*" *South Central Review* 21.3 (Fall): 150–68.

Benito, Jesús, and Ana Manzanas. "Border(lands) and Border Writing: Introductory Essay." In *Literature and Ethnicity in the Cultural Borderlands.* Ed. Jesús Benito and Ana Manzanas. Amsterdam: Rodopi, 2002. 1–24.

Bordwell, David. *Poetics of Cinema.* New York: Routledge, 2008.

———. *The Way Hollywood Tells It: Story and Style in Modern Movies.* Berkeley: University of California Press, 2006.

Bosley, Rachael K. "Forging Connections." *American Cinematographer* 87.11 (November 2006); accessed April 13, 2009. http://www.ascmag.com/magazine_dynamic/November2006/Babel/page1.php.

Calhoun, John. "Heartbreak and Loss." *American Cinematographer* 84.12 (December 2003); accessed March 30, 2009. http://www.ascmag.com/magazine/dec03/cover/index.html.

Cameron, Allan. "Contingency, Order, and the Modular Narrative: *21 Grams* and *Irreversible.*" *The Velvet Light Trap* 58 (Fall 2006): 65–78.

Cantú, Norma Elia. "Interview with Jorge Mariscal." *UCSD Guestbook* (1998); accessed March 16, 2009. http://www.youtube.com/watch?v=4DGQks2Uwvc.

Castells, Manuel. *The Rise of the Network Society.* 2nd ed. Oxford: Blackwell, 2000.

Certeau, Michel de. *The Practice of Everyday Life.* Trans. Steven Randall. Berkeley: University of California Press, 1984.

Christie, Ian. "The Caretaker." *Sight and Sound* 19.6 (June 2009): 33.

Christopher, James. "The Real Hound Inspector." *The Times (London)*, May 17, 2001, 15.

Denby, David. "The New Disorder: Adventures in Film Narrative." *New Yorker,* March 5, 2007, 80–85.

D'Lugo, Marvin. "*Amores Perros/Love's a Bitch.*" In *The Cinema of Latin America.* Ed. Alberto Elena and Marina Díaz López. New York: Wallflower Press, 2004. 221–29.

Everett, Wendy. "Fractal Films and the Architecture of Complexity." *Studies in European Cinema* 2.3 (Winter 2005): 159–71.

Ezra, Elizabeth, and Terry Rowden. "General Introduction: What Is Transnational Cinema?" In *Transnational Cinema: The Film Reader.* Ed. Elizabeth Ezra and Terry Rowden. London: Routledge, 2006. 1–12.

———. "Introduction to Part Three." In *Transnational Cinema: The Film Reader.* Ed. Elizabeth Ezra and Terry Rowden. London: Routledge, 2006. 109–10.

———, eds. *Transnational Cinema: The Film Reader.* London: Routledge, 2006.

Fein, Seth. "Transcultural Anticommunism: Cold War Hollywood in Postwar Mexico." In *Visible Nations: Latin American Cinema and Video.* Ed. Chon Noriega. Minneapolis: University of Minnesota Press, 2000. 82–111.

Fojas, Camilla. *Border Bandits: Hollywood on the Southern Frontier.* Austin: University of Texas Press, 2008.

Foster, David William. *Mexico City in Contemporary Mexican Cinema.* Austin: University of Texas Press, 2002.

Foucault, Michel. *The History of Sexuality.* Vol. 1. Trans. Robert Hurley. Harmondsworth: Penguin, 1976.

Fregoso, Rosa Linda. *MeXicana Encounters: The Making of Social Identities on the Borderlands.* Berkeley: University of California Press, 2003.

García Canclini, Néstor. *Culturas híbridas: Estrategias para entrar y salir de la modernidad.* 2d. ed. Buenos Aires: Paidós, 2001.

———. "Will There Be Latin American Cinema in the Year 2000? Visual Culture in a Postnational Era." In *Framing Latin American Cinema.* Ed. Ann Marie Stock. Minneapolis: University of Minnesota Press, 1997. 246–58.

García, Rodrigo. "The Foundations of *Babel*: A Conversation between Rodrigo García and Alejandro González Iñárritu." In *Babel: A Film by Alejandro González Iñárritu.* Ed. María Hargerman. Hong Kong: Taschen, 2007. 256–63.

Goldin, Nan. *The Ballad of Sexual Dependency.* New York: Aperture, 1986.

González Gutiérrez, Carlos. "Fostering Identities: Mexico's Relations with Its Diaspora." *Journal of American History* 86.2 (September 1999): 545–67.

Gutiérrez, Natividad. "Arquetipos y estereotipos en la construcción de la identidad nacional de México." *Revista Mexicana de Sociología* 60.1 (January–March 1998): 81–90.

Hahn, Robert. "*21 Grams.*" *Film Quarterly* 58.3 (March 2005): 53–58.

Hershfield, Joanne. "Mexico." In *The International Movie Industry.* Ed. Gorham Kinden. Carbondale: Southern Illinois University Press, 2000. 273–91.

Hershfield, Joane, and David R. Maciel. Epilogue to *Mexico's Cinema: A Century of Film and Filmmakers.* Ed. Joane Hershfield and David R. Maciel. Lanham, Md.: SR Books, 2005. 287–91.

Hirschberg, Lynn. "A New Mexican." *New York Times Magazine,* March 18, 2001, 32–35.

Hoberman, J. "Heaven Can Weight." *Village Voice,* November 19–25, 2003, 64.

Kerr, Sarah. "The Rules of Attraction." *Vogue,* November 2003, 352–54.

Krauze, Enrique. "*21 Grams.*" *Los Angeles Times,* February 22, 2004.

Kun, Josh. "The Sun Never Sets on MTV: Tijuana NO! and the Border of Music Video." In *Latino/a Popular Culture.* Ed. Michelle Habell Pallán and Mary Romero. New York: New York University Press, 2002. 102–13.

Landesman, Cosmo. "Hardly Worth the Weight." *Sunday Times (London),* March 7, 2004, 15.

Latour, Bruno. *Reassembling the Social: An Introduction to Actor-Network Theory.* Oxford: Oxford University Press, 2005.

Littger, Stephan. *The Director's Cut: Picturing Hollywood in the 21st Century.* New York: Continuum, 2006.

López, Ana M. "Crossing Nations and Genres: Traveling Filmmakers." In *Visible Nations: Latin American Cinema and Video.* Ed. Chon Noriega. Minneapolis: University of Minnesota Press, 2000. 33–50.

Lowenstein, Stephen. *My First Movie, Take Two: Ten Celebrated Directors Talk about Their First Film.* New York: Pantheon, 2008.

Maciel, David R. *El Norte: The U.S.–Mexican Border in Contemporary Cinema.* San Diego: Institute for Regional Studies of the Californias, San Diego State University, 1990.

Menne, Jeff. "A Mexican *Nouvelle Vague*: The Logic of New Waves under Globalization." *Cinema Journal* 47.1 (Fall 2007): 70–92.

Mora, Carl J. *Mexican Cinema: Reflections of a Society, 1896–2004.* 3d ed. Jefferson, N.C.: McFarland, 2005.

Mora, Sergio de la. *Cinemachismo, Masculinities, and Sexuality in Mexican Film.* Austin: University of Texas Press, 2006.

Morales, Ed. "Pulp Nonfiction." *The Village Voice,* April 3, 2001, 126.

Muñoz, Lorenza. "Modern Mexico Unleashed." *Los Angeles Times,* April 8, 2001, 10, 23–28.

Naficy, Hamid. "Situating Accented Cinema." In *Transnational Cinema: The Film Reader.* Ed. Elizabeth Ezra and Terry Rowden. London: Routledge, 2006. 111–29.

Naremore, James. *On Kubrick.* London: British Film Institute, 2007.

Neupert, Richard. *The End: Narration and Closure in the Cinema.* Detroit: Wayne State University Press, 1995.

Niogret, Hubert. "Aller au fond des choses" (Interview with Alejandro González Iñárritu). *Positif* 477 (November 2000): 24–28.

Noble, Andrea. *Mexican National Cinema.* London: Routledge, 2005.

Noriega, Chon. Introduction to *Visible Nations: Latin American Cinema and Video.* Ed. Chon Noriega. Minneapolis: University of Minnesota Press, 2000. xi–xxv.

———, ed. *Visible Nations: Latin American Cinema and Video.* Minneapolis: University of Minnesota Press, 2000.

Paz, Octavio. *El laberinto de la soledad.* 1950; reprint, Madrid: Cátedra, 2003.

Pratt, Mary Louise. *Imperial Eyes: Travel Writing and Transculturation.* London: Routledge, 1992.

Quart, Alissa. "*21 Grams.*" *Film Comment* 39.6 (November/December 2003): 74.

Ramírez Berg, Charles. *Cinema of Solitude: A Critical Study of Mexican Film, 1967–1983.* Austin: University of Texas Press, 1992.

Rich, B. Ruby. "Mexico at the Multiplex." *The Nation,* May 14, 2001, 34–36.

Romney, Jonathan. "Buy One Mexican Film, Get Two More Free." *The Independent on Sunday,* May 20, 2001.

———. "Enigma Variations." *Sight and Sound* 14.3 (March 2004): 12–16.

———. "Emotional Order" (Interview with Alejandro González Iñárritu). *Sight and Sound* 14.3 (March 2004): 15.

Saldaña-Portillo, María Josefina. "In the Shadow of NAFTA: *Y tu mamá también* Revisits the National Allegory of Mexican Sovereignty." *American Quarterly* 57.3 (September 2005): 751–77.

Schaefer, Claudia. *Bored to Distraction.* Albany: State University of New York Press, 2003.

Scott, Kevin Conroy. *Screenwriters' Masterclass: Screenwriters Talk about Their Greatest Movies.* New York: Newmarket Press, 2006.

Shohat, Ella. "Post-Third-Worldist Culture: Gender, Nation, and Cinema." In *Transnational Cinema: The Film Reader.* Ed. Elizabeth Ezra and Terry Rowden. London: Routledge, 2006. 39–56.

Smith, Paul Julian. *Amores Perros.* London: British Film Institute, 2003.

————. "Tower of Babel." *Sight and Sound* 19.3 (March 2009): 96.

Stock, Ann Marie. "Authentically Mexican? *Mi Querido Tom Mix* and *Cronos* Reframe Critical Questions." In *Mexico's Cinema: A Century of Film and Filmmakers*. Ed. Joane Hershfield and David R. Maciel. Lanham, Md.: SR Books, 2005. 267–87.

————. "Migrancy and the Latin American Cinemascape: Towards a Post-National Critical Praxis." In *Transnational Cinema: The Film Reader*. Ed. Elizabeth Ezra and Terry Rowden. London: Routledge, 2006. 157–65.

Tröhler, Margrit. *Offene Welten ohne Helden: Plurale Figurenkonstellationen im Film*. Marburg: Schüren, 2007.

Tuan, Yi-Fu. *Space and Place: The Perspective of Experience*. Minneapolis: University of Minnesota Press, 1977.

Tzioumakis, Yannis. *American Independent Cinema*. Edinburgh: Edinburgh University Press, 2006.

Wood, Jason. *The Faber Book of Mexican Cinema*. London: Faber and Faber, 2006.

Index

Celestino Deleyto is a professor of film and English literature at the University of Zaragoza, Spain, and author of *The Secret Life of Romantic Comedy* and others.

María del Mar Azcona is assistant professor of film at the University of Zaragoza and author of *The Multi-Protagonist Film*.

The University of Illinois Press
is a founding member of the
Association of American University Presses.

Designed by Paula Newcomb
Composed in 10/13 New Caledonia
with Helvetica Neue display
at the University of Illinois Press
Manufactured by Sheridan Books, Inc.

University of Illinois Press
1325 South Oak Street
Champaign, IL 61820-6903
www.press.uillinois.edu